COCKATOO
My Life in Cape York

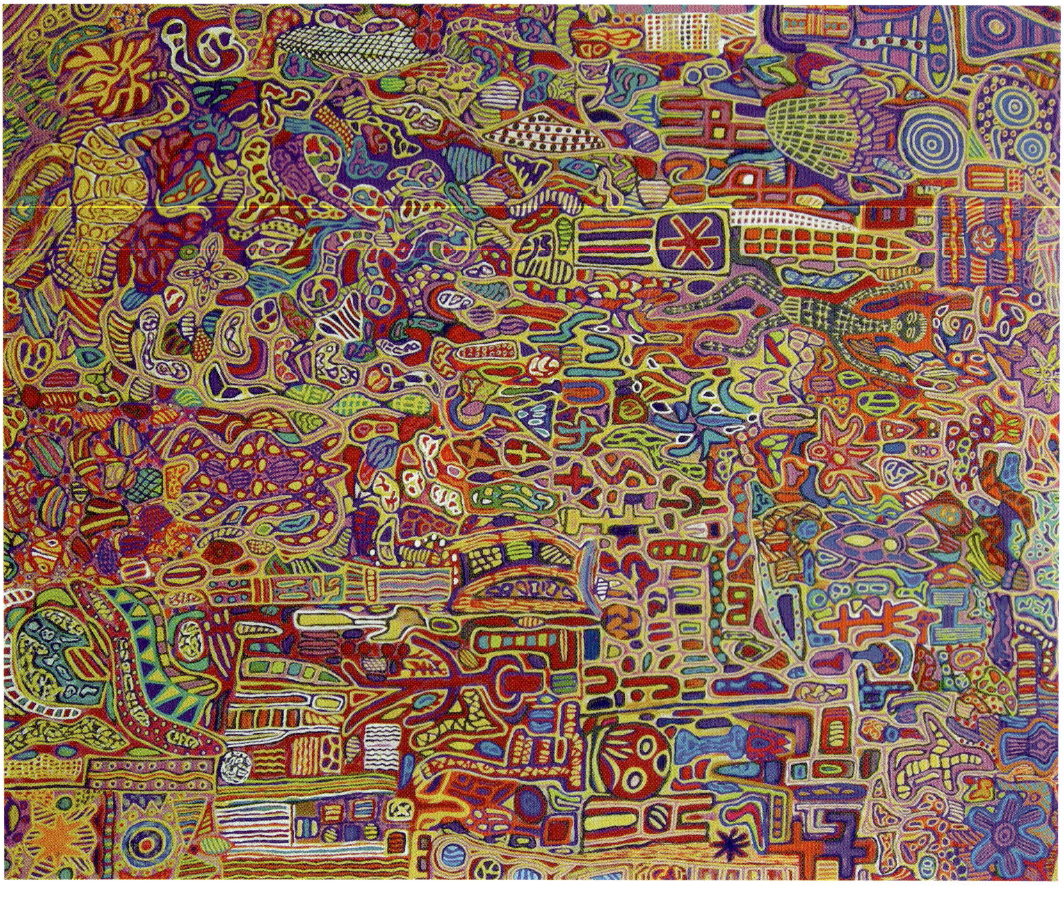

COCKATOO
My Life in Cape York

STORIES AND ART BY
ROY McIVOR

Magabala Books

First published 2010 by Magabala Books Aboriginal Corporation,
Broome, Western Australia
Website: www.magabala.com Email: sales@magabala.com

Magabala Books receives financial assistance from the Commonwealth Government through the Australia Council, its arts advisory body. The State of Western Australia has made an investment in this project through the Department of Culture and the Arts in association with Lotterywest.

Copyright © Text Roy McIvor, 2010
Copyright © for photographs belongs with the individual owners.

All rights reserved. Apart from any fair dealing for the purposes of private study, research, criticism or review, as permitted under the Copyright Act, no part of this publication may be reproduced by any process whatsoever without the written permission of the author, the illustrator and the publisher.

Cover design Mark Thacker, Big Cat Design
Internal design Bronwyn Houston
Printed in China at Everbest Printing Company

Cataloguing-in-Publication data is available from the National Library of Australia

CAPTIONS
Endpapers: 'Maji bithaaygu buliili' #1, Raindrops 1, 2007
Front cover and page 5: 'Wandarr, ngurraarr',
White cockatoo, black cockatoo, 2000
Page 2: Dynamic order #4, 2009
Page 9: 'Birra gurra walngangay', Homeland river lagoon, 2006

To my father Paddy McIvor whose wisdom, honour and love inspired me. To my mother Rachel McIvor whose love, care and teaching has sustained me. To my brother and sisters who were always there for me. To my dear wife Thelma and my very special children, Ramona, Selwyn and Elroy, of whom I am very proud. And to all my people who have walked this journey with me.

North of Cooktown

Starcke River
Point Lookout
Cape Flattery
Silica Sand Mine
Starcke station
Glenrock station
Mt Webb
Elderslie Station
Mt Baird
Morgan River
Wayarego
McIvor River
Cape Bedford
Elim
Hope Valley
HopeVale
Nob Point
Indian Head
Spring Hill
Mt Saunders
Endeavour River
Cooktown

Coen
Cooktown
Cairns
Charters Towers
Mount Isa
Stonehenge
Rockhampton
Woorabinda
Brisbane

Queensland

This story takes place in the coastal region of Cape York in far north Queensland. I was born on the Lutheran mission at Hope Valley, twenty-five kilometres north of Cooktown in 1934. I am a Guugu Yimithirr man.

The Guugu Yimithirr nation is made up of thirty-two clan groups. The clans are divided into two moiety groups, distinguished by the white and black cockatoos, wandarr and ngurraarr. My family are Binthi-warra (belonging to the Binthi clan). We are wandarr, or white cockatoo people. Our land extends from Redbank, south of the McIvor River, north to the Morgan River.

Today, the black and white cockatoos are a symbol of respect and cooperation between traditional social groups. In a wider context, they can be seen to represent our desire to live harmoniously together, as black and white Australians. The basis of this way of living together is respect. Black and white Australians have so much they can learn and share with each other.

I can identify with the symbolism of the black and white cockatoos, as my life has embraced two different worlds. I was lucky enough to have been taught many of the traditional ways of the Guugu Yimithirr people by my father, my uncles and many of the grand old people I lived amongst. I was brought up speaking my own language. As a child, I learned about my own country, its birds, fish, animals and plants. I was also a child of the mission, and learned about the Christian faith. I saw the Lutheran Church as the friend and supporter of our people.

As a young man, I had experience of the wider world. I learned my trade as a builder, craftsman and artist, and felt I could mix easily and happily with whoever crossed my path. Marriage with Thelma has confirmed this easy mix of cultures. I see this merging of black and white as the true future of our country. We can all share in the good things each side has to offer.

I hope you enjoy my story.

Roy McIvor, 2009

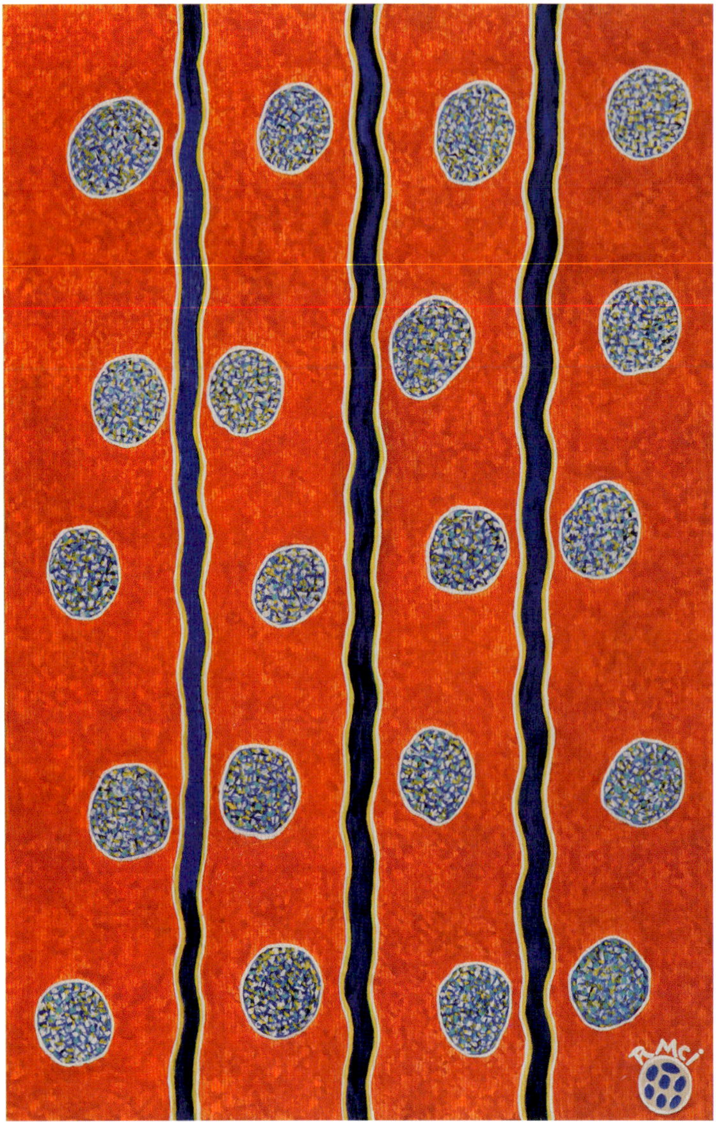

CONTENTS

PROLOGUE	Nellie and King Johnny	13
ONE	Journey to Hope Valley	21
TWO	Family life	35
THREE	Spring Hill	49
FOUR	Prisoners of war	71
FIVE	Years in exile	85
SIX	My people want to go home	107
SEVEN	Establishing Hope Vale	117
EIGHT	Sing a song of love	133
NINE	Call to church	145
TEN	Return to Hope Vale	159
ELEVEN	My art and my story	169
GUUGU YIMITHIRR GLOSSARY		175
ACKNOWLEDGEMENTS		176

'Bayji', Dilly bag, 2007

I remember our old ladies always being so busy. As a child I saw them making dilly bags and using them in different ways. All young girls were taught the process of making these special bags.

Culturally they were a necessity for carrying things in and they were used for special practices, such as leaching toxins from foods to make them edible. The making of dilly bags has begun to emerge again. It is a specialised women's craft, a woman's mark of cultural pride and a symbol of traditional life.

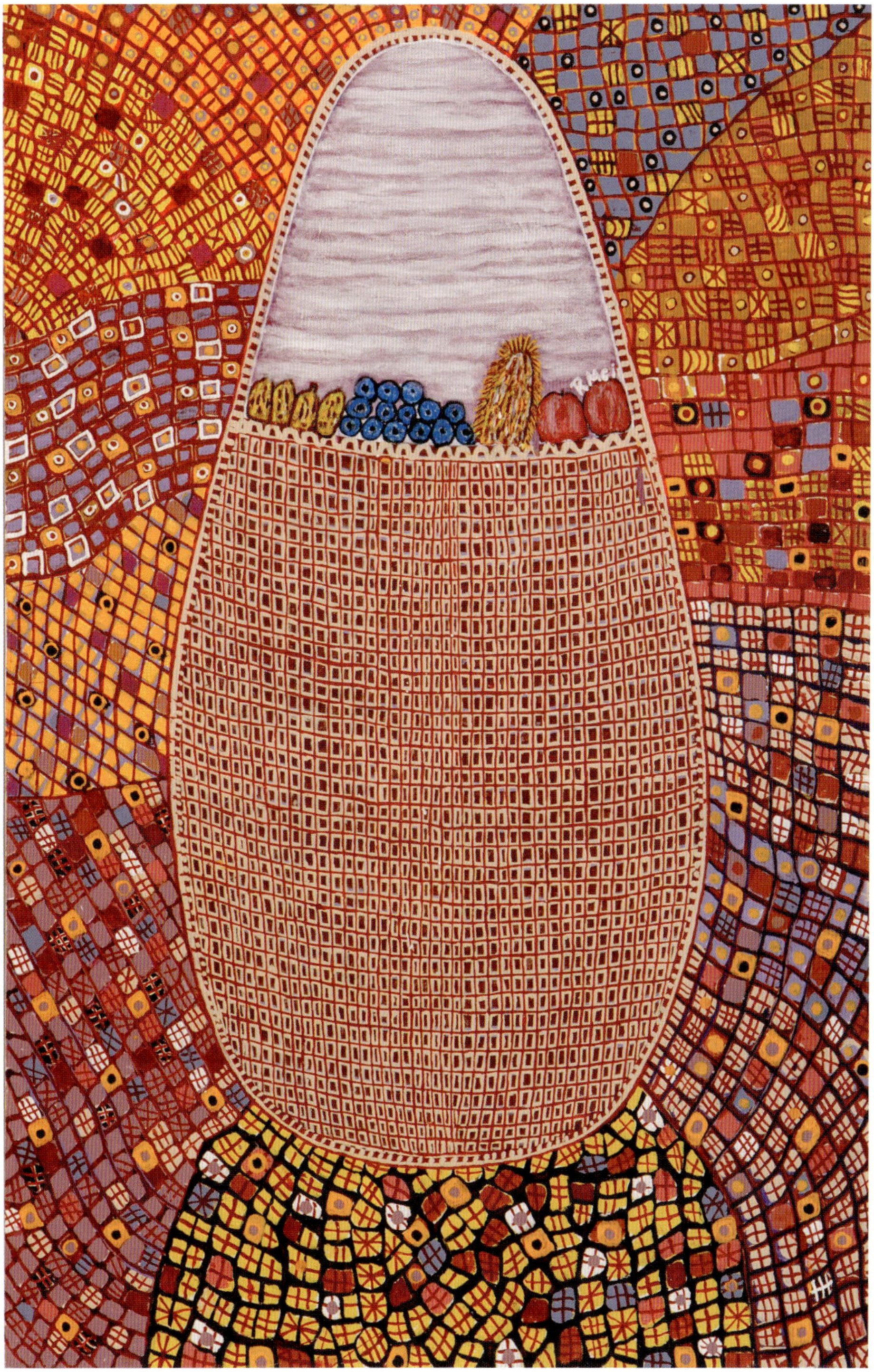

'Different solutions to violence', Thelma McIvor

My father took me to the place on the south side of the McIvor River where the Elderslie Stationers confronted the Binthi camp. He took me to show me the fig tree where his mother, Nellie, had hidden him. It had fallen down but another, where others had sheltered, was still there.

PROLOGUE

Nellie and King Johnny

My father, Munarra (Paddy), was born around 1897. His tribal father was King Johnny of the Binthi clan from the McIvor River area. Munarra's white father was a yard-builder from Glenrock Station. He lived in the area only a short time.

Munarra's mother was Nuungaal (Nellie). She had a sister called Jingulu (Maudie) who was the mother of Woibo. Both Nuungaal and Jingulu were the wives of King Johnny.

Munarra was Nuungaal's eldest son, and Batharra (Willie Wallace) his younger brother. Munarra and Batharra were taken to live on the Hope Valley Lutheran mission at Cape Bedford when they were young boys. There may have been a younger son who was named Jack Wallace. Some years ago, a lady from Tasmania told us that she was my niece and the granddaughter of Jack Wallace. Jack was born after my father and Willie had gone to live at Hope Valley. He was later adopted by the sergeant of police in Cooktown, and moved to Mareeba.

Since the late 1800s, Aboriginal people in the region had co-existed with the white settlers. They moved around their traditional country, and those who set up camps on the stations were expected to do jobs in return. In 1916, when King Johnny and Nellie were on Elderslie Station, they went hunting and burnt a patch of grass to clear out some game. The boss' wife saw the smoke and questioned the bama to find out who the culprits were. She reported King Johnny and Nellie to the Cooktown police who came and took them away on a buckboard (a four-wheeled horse-drawn wagon). They were sent from Cooktown to Townsville by boat, and then by train to Brisbane. From there they were sent to the Aboriginal Reserve at Barambah (now known as Cherbourg) where Nellie later died.

After Nellie died, the old man decided to walk back to his country. He had a keen sense of direction and eventually made it back to Cooktown, more than 1800 kilometres away. His people were surprised to see him. They said, 'You have been away a long time, we thought you were dead.' Someone took him back to North Shore by canoe. Everyone was glad to see him.

Uncle Willie was on the river bank with Bob Flinders, and thought he heard his father's voice. Bob laughed at him and told him that was impossible as he was far away down south. But Willie insisted and, sure enough, it was his father who had just walked all the way home from Barambah.

When my father was much older, he met an old lady at Woorabinda. Her name was Maudie Clark. He started telling her about King Johnny and she said: 'The old fella who walked back from Cherbourg? I was working at Biloela on a cattle station, and one evening before sunset, I saw a lone figure coming up the road. He walked right up to where I was, and when he got close, I asked him, "Old fella, where are you going?" "I am going back to Cooktown," he replied. The station owners had gone to Biloela to get supplies. I told him he could camp there, and I cooked him damper. Before he left I gave him a bag with some flour, sugar and tea. He had a long way to walk. He did not know how to thank me, he was very grateful.'

Tribal Kings

In the early years of the twentieth century, 'Kings' were appointed by white authorities among the coastal tribes on Cape York. They were presented with brass breast-plates as symbols of their authority, and were called on to cooperate with missionaries, police and government representatives. The government issued blankets and clothing to the kings, who distributed these items among their clan group. In 1911, King-plates were given to men of the Guugu Yimithirr nation, including my grandfather, King Johnny.

King Jacko, with bama from the Dyunydu clan

King Jacko lived peacefully close to the mission. He had good relations with Muni, who relied on him to keep the roads in good order and to report any illegal activities.

Cherbourg

Cherbourg, 280 kilometres northwest of Brisbane, is one of the largest Aboriginal communities in Queensland. It was founded in 1901 when the Queensland Government set aside 7,000 acres as an Aboriginal reserve – it was then known as the Barambah Aboriginal Reserve.

In the early days, there were two cattle stations in my father's tribal area, owned by white families. Bama used to camp at a place on the south side of the McIvor River. One day, the station owners and their sons rode into the camp on their horses, whipping everyone they could find with their stock whips, breaking the spears and dilly bags and throwing them in the river. Men, women and children scattered in terror. Even women and old people were not spared.

Babi Nellie hid with my father and Willie in a buttress of a fig tree. Finally old man Stumpy, who was from a neighbouring clan and had been visiting the camp, faced the wangaarr (white person) with his fighting spears and threatened them. The wangaarr were terrified and fled. Old man Stumpy must have been a great warrior, and he certainly must have looked frightening enough to scare these men off!

My father heard the story of this massacre from Ngamu Wuthurru, who escaped from the site, and from another survivor, William Daku, a Waymbuurr-warra man, who was a ten-year-old boy at the time.

Trackers

Sergeant Kenny was in charge of the native police who were based down at Marton. Many of these police were skilled trackers from Fraser Island further south, and crack shots. Under Kenny's leadership, the trackers travelled up the coast to participate in the massacres. My father said Kenny was an expert marksman and could shoot a bird in flight.

When he retired, Kenny came to Hope Valley with his daughter. He was an engineer and Muni employed him to work the sisal hemp plantation. He laid out the cement bed for the steam engine used in the processing, and it is still there today. Kenny went on to the mission at Hull River, north of Tully, and he and his daughter died in the 1907 cyclone that destroyed the mission.

Captain Robert Watson was a bêche-de-mer fisherman who was working off Lizard Island. When the island was attacked and one of his servants was killed, his wife tried to escape with their only child and another servant in an iron boiling tank. The tank drifted and all three died. Afterwards there were reprisal killings by white troopers and native police on the mainland. There were killings right up the coast. Sleeping bama were surprised by bulimun (police) at Connie's Beach, north of Cape Flattery. Others were massacred at Yuwaal-bitha (small beach), which is where you will find the new jetty at Cape Flattery today. Another massacre happened at Normanby. People were given flour, sugar and tea poisoned with arsenic. They died a terrible death.

We were aware of the sad history of the place. I saw skulls and bones in a rock shelf at Binirrigu (north of Cape Bedford) and at the top of the sandhills north of the mouth of the McIvor River. Skulls and bones were also found at Jarwigu (east of Elim).

Trial by spearing

In the old days, when there was an argument or misdemeanour to be settled, messages on a message stick were sent to the tribes involved. Ceremonial grounds were usually located in neutral areas, and arguments were settled by the ritual defence of the mala-digarra. The mala-digarra were warriors who acted as lawyers for the accused. When the bama were assembled, the mala-digarra would gather with the accused man behind them. The prosecuting bama would then hurl spears at them from a distance, which the mala-digarra would deflect with a woomera. As the prosecutors came closer, the trial became more dangerous. If the accused was not injured, the case would be dropped and no further action taken.

In my father's day, Butchin and Gunguunbi were both champion mala-digarra. They were formidable hunters and highly respected.

Risen from the dead

The Guuthi sandhills are part of Binthi country. One time, Uncle Willie was desperately ill near the salt-pans on the eastern side of Guuthi. He was with Michael Charlie, Fred Jacko, Charlie Pearson and Monty Woibo. These men thought that Willie was going to die. He asked to be taken to the streamlet running from the freshwater lake and washed himself with the water. The others were getting ready to dig his grave! Then he asked them to carry him up to the top of the sand hill. They couldn't believe their ears, as he seemed too ill. It was a steep climb, but Willie insisted. They carried him halfway and then put him down. He forced them to continue the trip, all the way to the top. There Willie turned this way and that. He was there for some time, and seemed to be in deep communication. Then he turned and came down the hill like a young man, completely restored to health. The would-be grave diggers were amazed.

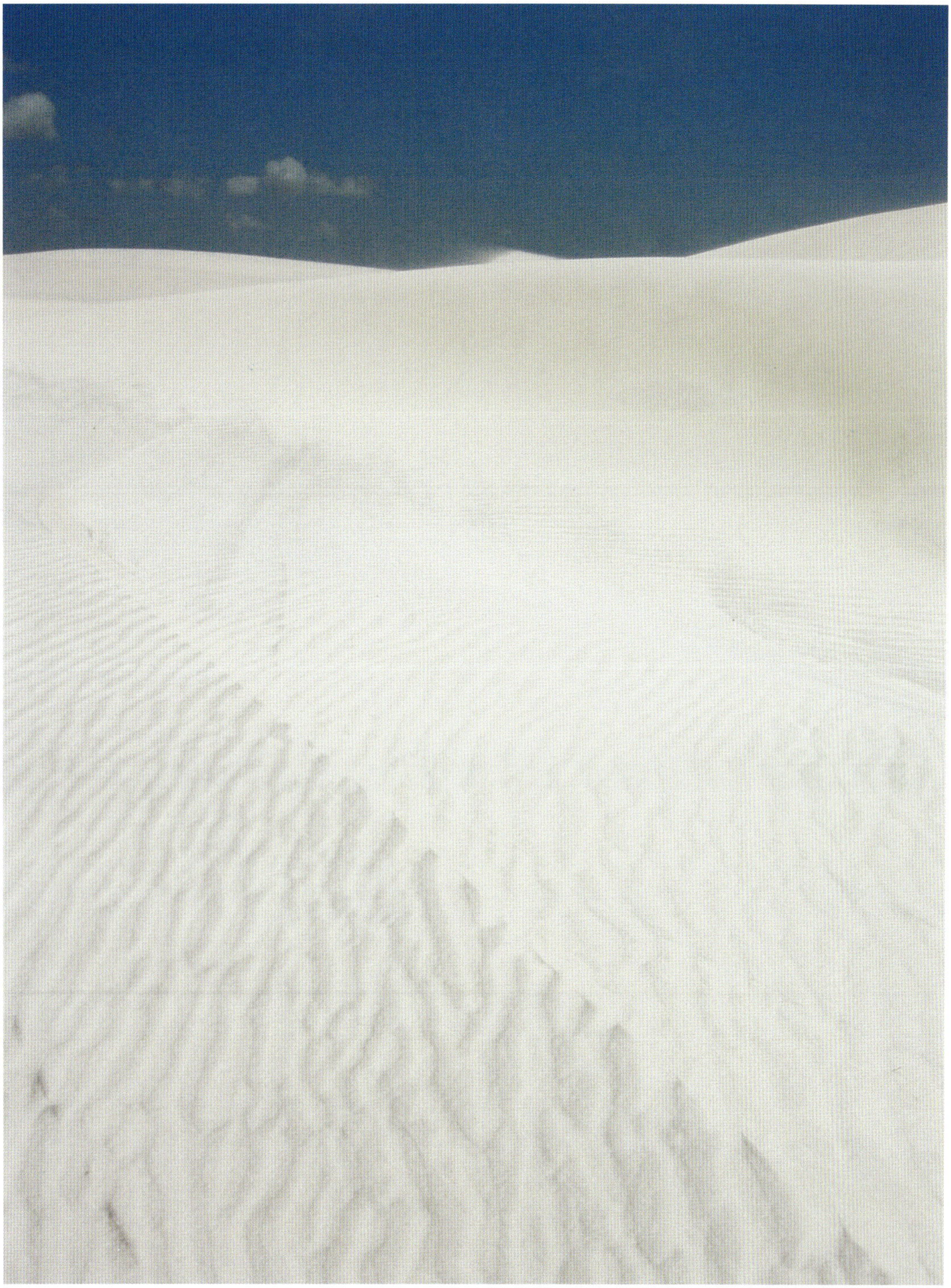

Aerial view of Hope
Valley Mission, Cape
Bedford, c. 1930

CHAPTER ONE

Journey to Hope Valley

In the 1870s, Guugu Yimithirr tribes were severely affected by the establishment of Cooktown as a hub for the Palmer River goldrush. Our traditional land was seized for farming and to establish the pearl shell, trochus and trepang industries along the coast.

By the beginning of the twentieth century, many of our women had been forced into relationships with white men or raped. Their children were taken away. This immoral behaviour turned our culture upside down. Family traditions and marriage lines were broken and the effects of this are felt to this day.

The impact of this invasion of Far North Queensland has never been fully acknowledged, and the survival of the our people and the preservation of our language was due to the establishment of the Hope Valley mission in 1886.

A temporary Aboriginal Reserve had been set up on the North Shore in 1879, and extended in 1881. In 1885, Johannes Flierl was on his way to New Guinea when he arrived in Cooktown.

He saw the need for a mission, and wrote to the South Australian Lutheran Synod. In 1886, a Lutheran mission was established at Elim Beach and Missionary Meyer, his wife and Johannes Pingilina were sent to replace Missionary Flierl. Johann Pfalzar travelled from Germany to join them later that year.

The first children to come to the mission were girls from the surviving local clan groups. They were the first converts to Christianity. Then young men seeking wives joined them. By the first years of the twentieth century, children were sent from areas as far north as Injinoo and as far south as Stonehenge. Others were brought to the mission by their parents, in desperation at no longer being able to care for them.

All children were accepted by bama, and dagaarr manaa (adoption) by families was a common practice. The boys and young men in the dormitories often adopted newcomers as their brother or son. Uncle Roy Dick was adopted into our family, and this is how he became a brother to my father. That relationship lasted for life.

Living under the Act

The notorious Queensland Aboriginals Protection and Restriction of the Sale of Opium Act of 1897, gave the government control over every aspect of the lives of Aboriginal people. The Protector and the Welfare Boards decided where they would live, who they could marry, who they could mix with, and how they looked after their children. Housing and diet were controlled, and the government decided where they could travel and who could visit them. Authorities dictated what jobs Aboriginal people were allowed to do and under what conditions, and how much they could receive as wages. This legislation lasted until the 1970s.

Exemption from the Act was offered to selected Indigenous men and their families. It was an unreliable benefit, as it involved renouncing one's Aboriginality, and it could be withdrawn at any time. I think today's Welfare Reform mirrors many aspects of 'living under the Act'. It is simply history repeated.

Journey to Hope Valley

Missionary George Schwarz (Muni)

Missionary Schwarz arrived at Cape Bedford in 1887. He was only nineteen years old and had sailed from Cooktown in the 'Rabbit'.

Muni's wife, Mary Allen Schwarz, and mission school children

Mary Allen Schwarz arrived via Allen Point, which was later named in her honour.

Marriage guidance

When the first school teacher arrived from Cooktown, she was young, fair and pretty. Muni went to the old women and asked them their opinion of her as a possible wife. 'No, no! She won't do for you as a wife.' In time she was replaced by another teacher, Mary Allen. Her parents ran the Post Office in Cooktown and her sisters were qualified nurses who served overseas in the war. Muni went back to the old ladies and asked their opinion of this girl. 'Yes. Yes!' they said. 'This one will do very nicely for you.' And so it turned out.

Missionary Schwarz, affectionately known as 'Muni', arrived in 1887. Schwarz is the German word for 'black' and Muni means 'black' in Guugu Yimithirr. The mission was moved to Cape Bedford on 19 December 1887. In time, the other missionaries left but Muni remained until his retirement more than fifty years later. Muni was an authoritarian figure who was loved and respected by the Guugu Yimithirr people. However, not all bama supported the mission way of life. Muni's policy was to keep the mission people in isolation, away from the neighbouring stations. Traditional dancing, singing and ceremonies were forbidden on the mission site, although Muni did have a good relationship with the bama who lived at Bridge Creek and he often worked with them. Muni also valued speaking and translating Guugu Yimithirr and he had an important role in preserving the language.

Muni was not always made welcome. Soon after his arrival, spears were thrown at him when he was walking along the beach, but he remained calm and was not hurt. Some time later, Muni was riding a horse along a solitary track when two old warriors appeared silently before him. He stopped his horse and sat still while they came up to him and quietly ran their hands along his bare legs, pausing at the fleshy bits, and making appreciative eating noises. They disappeared into the bush and Muni rode on, feeling rather relieved.

When Dad was a young boy, he was with his cousin/brother Woibo and other boys at a nganyja (initiation) ceremony at the Muuwuntha waterholes on the McIvor River. They were in training to become nguumbaal (initiated man).

When Dad went through his initiation ceremony, he travelled up north to a place on the Starcke River with the other initiates and some Elders, where they made a camp. Guyumughu and his wife were with them. Guyumughu was showing his skills at spearing a ganhaarr (crocodile). He took the boys to a lagoon, where he dived into the water with two spears and speared a crocodile through the soft underarm. When he came up, he told the boys to wait for the ganhaarr to come floating up. When the ganhaarr surfaced, they got it out of the water and took it back to the camp, where they cooked it up in a gurma (underground oven). Dad said he loved the taste of ganhaarr minha (meat).

Muni came out from the mission at Cape Bedford to collect the boys. He waited for the ceremony to end, and discussed his intentions with the Elders to take the boys to the mission. The Elders agreed that he could take them after they had finished the ceremony. This was the last initiation ceremony that was carried out by my people in the area. At this ceremony, the traditional practice of piercing the nose and scarring the body was not performed.

Nganyja (Initiation)

Initiation was carried out at puberty and marked the passage from childhood to adulthood. Initiates were tested in obedience, respect for their Elders, and self-control. For young men, the piercing of the nose or scarring on the chest were signs that they were initiated and carried authority. They now had the status of nguumbaal (initiated men), and were qualified to pass on to the next stage of their education.

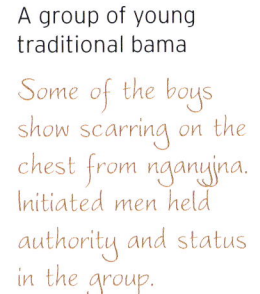

A group of young traditional bama

Some of the boys show scarring on the chest from nganyjna. Initiated men held authority and status in the group.

Cockatoo

After my father was taken to the mission, he grew up living in the boys' dormitory. Dad went on to become a leading seaman, and worked on the first mission boat, the Pearl Queen. When the Ramona was bought, he became the ship's captain, and had Mugay Woibo, Uncle Willie and others as his crew. Dad always spoke highly of the men he worked with. As captain of the Ramona, he trained a generation of seamen who built the trade in trochus, bêche-de-mer and dugong oil. This trade was a significant factor in the economic survival of the mission.

Uncle Willie had avoided the mission for a good few years after his brother and cousin were taken. But one time, Muni told Dad, Mugay Woibo and Bapa Charlie Pearson to go down to Nguurru, the beach south of Cape Bedford, and wait to meet their relative. They set off with spears and a billycan and waited there, fishing, until a little group appeared coming round Nobby Point. Uncle Willie was with them and they all cried together. Then they set off for the mission, taking turns at carrying Uncle Willie on their shoulders.

Paddy McIvor

In 1908, my father, Munarra, was baptised and took the name of Paddy McIvor. Dad displayed leadership qualities from a young age, as he had early responsibilities. When he grew up, he was put in charge of the boys' dormitory. For some time it was my father who was the first bama to welcome many of the frightened little boys when they arrived at Cape Bedford.

Church congregation at Hope Valley. Ngathi Karl and his wife, Gami Louisa, are the first couple in the back row

Ngathi Karl was an evangelist and senior man. He was well-trusted by Muni.

Mugay Woibo and my father always referred to each other as brothers, which is common in our culture. Because they were taken to the mission together, they were as close as real brothers. Mugay Woibo was always known as an upright and reliable worker. He later married Lily Stuckey, a Balngaar woman. She was the daughter of a white man who was a close associate of Muni. Lily's father was the only white man to acknowledge his child at the mission, and he used to bring her presents at Christmas and other times.

Mugay Woibo and Mugay Lily first lived at Elim, and later at Spring Hill with their sons Monty, Willy and Francis. Their daughter, Kathleen, married not long after they moved to Spring Hill, and their other daughters, Margaret and Betty, lived in the girls' dormitory. Their youngest daughter Lily was born in Spring Hill. Mugay Lily died in 1942, and my mother and Aunty Dolly took care of little Lily. She was later adopted by Maudie Mulgal, the daughter of my grandmother's sister, Maggie.

My mother, Nellie Thompson, was born in 1902, in Stonehenge, near Longreach in Central Queensland. Her tribal name was Awaay. She had an older brother, Henry Kelly, and two younger siblings, Helen Thornton and Harold McGrath. Later, in 1913, when Mum and Helen were baptised, they changed their names to Rachel and Dolly respectively.

Mum's mother's name was Lizzie, and her Indigenous father's name was Jack. He worked as a stockman in the area of Stonehenge and died when Mum was only seven years old. It was a great loss to the family as he had worked hard to make ends meet.

Two white families in the area who helped during this time were the McGraths and the Kellys. The McGraths owned the Stonehenge Hotel. Lizzie worked there cleaning and doing laundry work, and the money she earned was enough to feed the family. The Chinese community at Stonehenge had gardens and they helped the family with fruit and vegetables.

Mum and Henry went to the Stonehenge school. They had a lot of relatives there, and would sometimes go on hunting trips for a day or two. They camped at the Thompson River, where they caught catfish and black bream. There was little rain; but sometimes it would rain out west causing flash floods to gush down the river, taking everyone by surprise. In the summer the ground split in the heat, and they found snakes in the cracks. I was told Uncle Henry was an excellent student. When he turned sixteen, he went to work as a stockman at Warbreccan Station, about fifty kilometres from Stonehenge.

After little Harold was born, Lizzie became ill. When she passed away, my great-grandmother looked after the children. She was working for Mrs Kelly, who kindly let the children stay at her house. At the time her husband lived out of town, where he kept horses and cattle. Sometimes on a weekend they'd go for long walks to visit Mr Kelly. I have always wondered if he was related to the famous bushranger Ned Kelly!

My great-grandmother used to play the piano accordion or the mouth organ for the shearers' dances. When she played, Mum, Helen and Harold went along and watched the people dance.

Unfortunately, Mrs Kelly died a few years later, in 1911, and a black tracker came for the children. He told their grandmother to

My mother, Rachel, (back row, third from the left) with other girls at Hope Valley, c. 1926

take them to the homestead. Here, they were told that they were being taken to school. Their grandmother objected, but it was no use. As they put the children on a Cobb & Co stage coach, she threw herself on the ground. When they looked back, the children saw their grandmother and other relatives rolling on the ground, wailing loudly. Nobody told them how far they would go, or where they were going. They thought they were going to the country near Winton, where they had family.

Mum told us later: 'I don't know how it happened that we ended up in the furthest Aboriginal mission.' Mum told the policeman that they wanted to say goodbye to their older brother at Warbreccan Station, and this was allowed. They drove to the station and said their teary goodbyes. Not knowing they were going so far away, Henry said, 'Don't worry, we will see each other again some day.' This never happened.

Mum said it was a long trip. She told me it took them about three weeks. It took several days to get to Hughenden. From there they caught a train to Townsville. Mum said they were surprised to see a train. They had never seen anything like it before! From Townsville they caught a boat, the 'Catalina', to Cooktown.

Cockatoo

There was no railway line between Townsville and Cairns at the time. This was also their first introduction to the big water!

After several days, they arrived in Cooktown and were taken to the police station. All this travelling had left them exhausted, and Mum said to Harold and Helen, 'I don't know how much further we have to go. We'll just have to wait and see what the police will tell us.' To their amazement, they met up with their cousin/sisters, Lizzie and Essie. Though taken from their families on separate occasions, they had now met up far from home. Lizzie and Essie had been separated from their brothers and would never see them again.

The police told them, 'Kids, you have travelled a long way, but you haven't got far to go now. You will leave on a sailing boat to go to a mission called Hope Valley at Cape Bedford. That's where you'll be looked after in a dormitory. The missionary in charge is a good man. His name is Mr Schwarz and his wife is the schoolteacher.'

At the dormitory, the children weren't strangers for long and soon made new friends. The other girls made them feel welcome, and so did Pastor and Mrs Schwarz. Mum and Aunty Dolly were amongst those working in the missionary's house. Mrs Schwarz picked the girls for her domestic work. They had to make the beds and learnt to be good cooks. The girls were strictly brought up learning God's word through the Bible. Mum told us how she sat many a time at the bedside of sick young girls, who were

The gates to Stonehenge

I didn't write down a lot of the stories Mum told us about her life at Stonehenge and I have forgotten many of them.

dying, and how each of them shared their visions of angels and Jesus coming to take them home.

It wasn't long before my mother, Dolly and Harold were adopted by the evangelist Ngathi Karl and his wife, Gami Louisa. Karl once went on a trip as an evangelist to Normanton and the Roper River with Deafy Wilkinson, an Anglican missionary.

I cannot remember my mother ever speaking one word of her language, Kunjkari, yet the children would have had to talk in their own language just after they arrived, as they could not yet speak Guugu Yimithirr. Mum's great bosom friends were Auntie Ann Cameron, Nguuthurr Lily Deeral and Auntie Maudie Mulgal. Auntie Dolly's great friends were Renee Deemal and Auntie Jenny Pearson. In their younger years, they were not allowed contact with people outside the mission.

Mum told us a lot of interesting stories about her earlier life at Stonehenge, but I never wrote them down and I have forgotten many of them, which I regret. My memories of my mother are mainly of her always being there, providing us with meals and clothes and comforting us when we felt hurt, ill or sad.

I do remember when Mum told me about playing on a big rock with some other girls. They were on the rock together and were competing to see who could stay on the longest. Mum lost her footing first and fell to the ground. The other girls, who had also lost their balance, landed on top of her. Mum came out of it with a broken rib. She did not receive any treatment, and had a lot of pain in later years. Dad used to treat her with heat packs made from warmed sand.

In 1960, some of the Hope Vale bama showed symptoms of tuberculosis and were sent to the hospital on Thursday Island for treatment. Mum was sent with them and stayed there for over a year. Later, in an X-ray, it was revealed that the broken rib could have caused an irritation to the lungs. Mum stayed on Thursday Island for seventeen months, until Dad went there to bring her home.

'Tree Kangaroo', 2007

One morning, Dad had been up Cape Bedford and came rushing back to get us. He sounded very excited, 'Come on, there is something up there that I want to show you!" So we all followed him eagerly. We went up the mountain and stopped near a tree. Up the tree, we saw a big gadaar yugumalin (Bennett's tree kangaroo) in very good shape. It was such a marvellous sight! My father didn't shoot it because they were rare. Dad often shot rock wallabies because they were abundant. They are small creatures, but they are good eating, and Mum would make a nice rock wallaby stew.

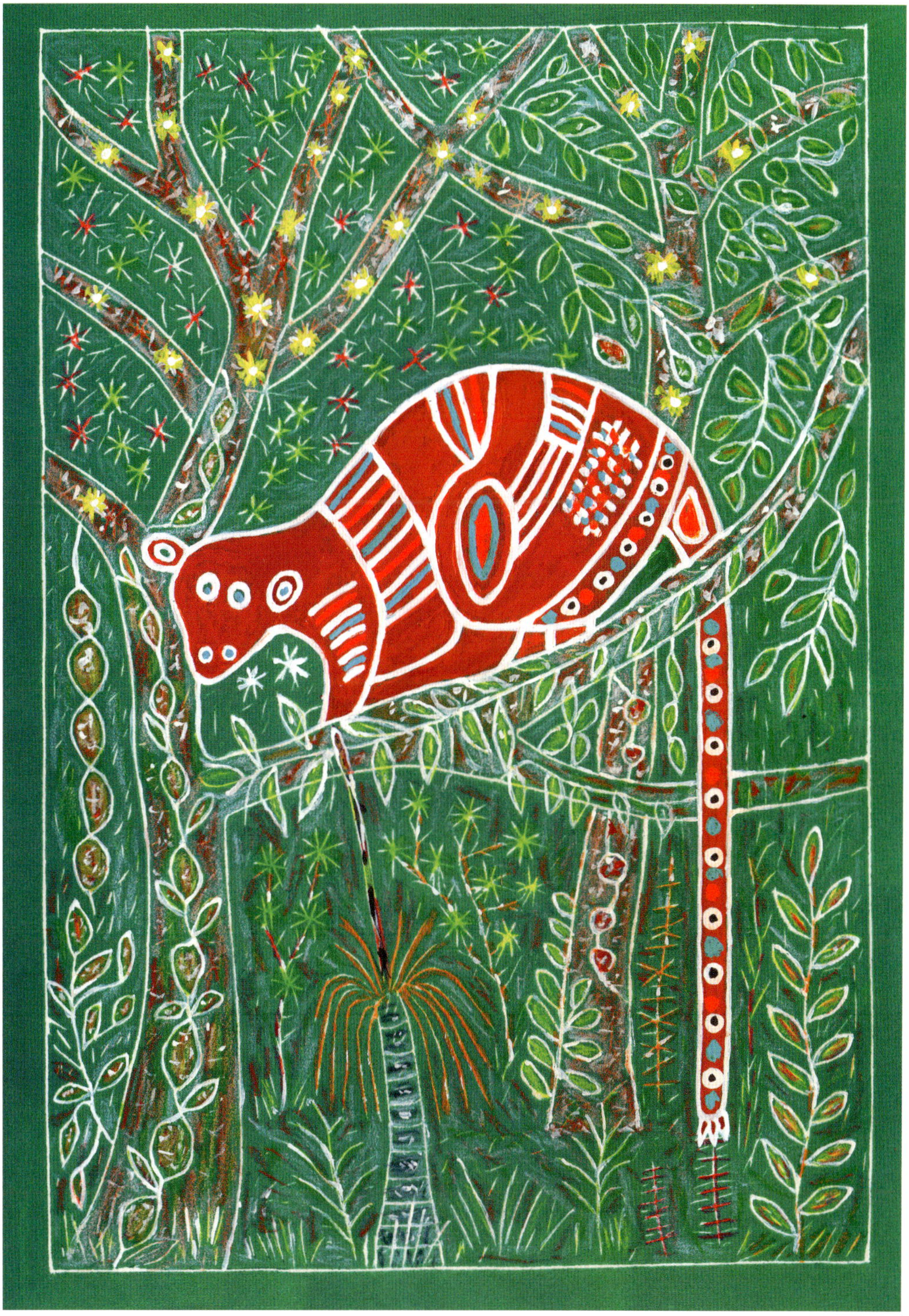

The beautiful coloured sands are about two kilometres from Elim

CHAPTER TWO

Family life

My mother Rachel and father Paddy met at the Hope Valley mission, and were married in 1927. Auntie Dolly married my Dad's younger brother, Willie. The couples moved to the mission outstation at Elim, the beach near the coloured sands, where they had houses next to each other. These houses were thatched with coconut fronds, and were cool and dry. Other bama lived in mission outstations at Ngaandalin, on the northern side of the McIvor River and Wayarego, on the southern side of the river.

Syd was born in 1930 and Emily was born in 1932. After Emily's birth, Muni asked Dad if my family could move back to Hope Valley. Dad told him he would ask Mum first, who said she'd only agree if Auntie Dolly and Uncle Willie could move there as well. This was fine by Muni. They all moved back to Hope Valley, where they lived for eight years.

My parents had three more children at Hope Valley. I was born in 1934, Ruth in 1936 and Dorothy in 1938. All in all, my parents had six children. Kathleen was the youngest. She was born in 1943 at Woorabinda.

Cockatoo

Midwives

In those days, women birthed their children at home. Gami Emma Capebedford, Gami Martha Muru and Nguuthurr Helena were skilled midwives. Apparently my head was out of shape after I was born. Gami Emma hit it several times and poked it with a warmed dhulgan (sheoak) leaf. My mother was worried about the treatment and protested, but Gami Emma persevered and succeeded. The shape of my head turned normal. In later years Gami Martha, Gami Emma and Nguuthurr Helena passed on their skills as midwives to Auntie Dolly and her friend Renee Deemal.

These three old ladies lived nearby to us and were part of my childhood. Gami Emma was a Guulaal-warra woman who married Jimmy Bandana, a Wundaal-warra man. Gami Martha was Daarba-warra, and one of the early Christians at the mission. Nguuthurr Helena was Ngatha-warra.

Auntie Dolly and Uncle Willie had nine children. Gertie and Pat were born at Elim. Lucy, Maud and Harold were born at Hope Valley. Dora was born at Spring Hill, but she died not long after. Auntie Dolly had her last two babies, Dora and Grace, in Woorabinda. They also adopted a son, Alan. Mum and Auntie Dolly were close and our families did everything together.

Life at Hope Valley seemed very good to me. There were a few buildings at the settlement: a house for the missionary, a school, a church, and the boys' and girls' dormitories. Some children were taken to the mission by parents who couldn't care for them, and others arrived after being forcibly removed from their traditional country by government authorities. It must have been hard for them to live there without their families. I was lucky to have mine. I felt loved and we had a lot more freedom, as the dormitory kids could not go out often.

Mum and Dad took us fishing, hunting and gathering bush tucker at Biniirrigu and Guguli. Dad used to take his rifle, and would often get a goanna or a wallaby on the way. Fishing lines were made of sisal hemp, which was shredded out and rolled between

Family life

Men and boys at Hope Valley. Paddy is standing, fifth man from the left

hand and leg until it was thin and strong. Only the hooks were bought in Cooktown. Sisal hemp was also used for weaving. The ladies wove it into tablemats, and then they dyed it with bush dye. The mats looked beautiful.

Emily, Syd and I loved fishing with Mum and Dad. Ruth and Dorothy were too small to join in, so Auntie Dolly minded them. Sometimes Mum would take the dormitory girls. They loved it; there was always someone who was lucky enough to catch a fish. Biniirrigu was good for hunting and fishing, and we loved to go swimming there on calm days. Another good area was Breakwater, where the beach ends at the southern side of Cape Bedford. As a young man, Missionary Muni took refuge in a cave at Breakwater after his long journey from Germany.

Sometimes Dad milked the mission cows, one of his many jobs, which I loved. I used to go and visit him in the morning. There would be a big bucket of milk, and he would bring it up to Muni. From there it was given out to the dormitories and the families. Muni also had a separator with which he made butter.

My father always had a close relationship with Muni. While never relinquishing his own authority, Muni trusted him and gave him responsibility. When Harry Bungurr was accused of leading other bama to break the law of the mission and go begging for tobacco on neighbouring stations, Muni decided to send him to Palm Island. Since 1918, Aboriginal and Islander people from throughout Queensland had been incarcerated at Palm Island, often for minor misdemeanours. Dad was related to Harry and a close friend of his brother, Dhabundhin. He urged Muni not to send him away. When Muni refused, Dad opposed him, almost to the point of fisticuffs. Years later, Muni musingly asked him, 'How far would you have gone, Paddy?' We never heard Dad's answer!

Each Sunday, bama would come all the way from Wayarego, Ngaandalin and Elim to attend church. Mugay Woibo and his family lived at Elim, and they walked over to Cape Bedford for the Sunday service. That was a great thing, having people walk long distances to attend church, bringing food for along the way. After the service, everyone walked back home again.

Muni would sit down with some of the old ladies who helped him translate his services into Guugu Yimithirr. He preached in either Guugu or English. Some hymns had been translated into Guugu Yimithirr and we sang them proudly. We still sing those hymns today and more have since been translated. Our bama had beautiful singing voices; I loved sitting around the campfire listening to them singing hymns in our own language. Their voices harmonised so well together. I really treasure these memories. Sometimes at Christmas the men would go out up the mountain

Gunbu Gunbu, Christmas

Christmas was a special time. Contact between traditional bama and converted bama at the mission was discouraged as it might interfere with the Christmas celebrations. During these festivities, the traditional bama were not allowed at the mission but they could camp on the beach. The sounds of carols sung in the mission church merged with the sounds of ganhil baathithil (traditional songs) from around the campfires on the beach.

A party at Elim. Mugay Woibo is the tall man on the left in the back row and Mugay Lily is seated in front

to gather ferns, singing along the way. They'd get a tree and the church would be beautifully decorated.

At Wayarego, Ngathi Karl held the services before a white pastor arrived. In 1928, Pastor Medingdorfer came from Germany. He married the following year, and he and his wife lived at Wayarego until 1932 when they had to move for health reasons. Pastor Medingdorfer held a service at Wayarego when the people could not make it to Cape Bedford, and he ran a mid-weekly service. Bama who had known the Medingdorfers said they were kind-hearted and good to the people.

Henry Deeral and I were not yet of school age, and had plenty of time for play with the other boys — Eric Deeral, George, Leonard and Lindsay Rosendale, Pat Wallace, Mulun Darkan, Syd, Emily and our cousin Gertie all went to school.

At times, we'd go up Cape Bedford mountain. On clear days you would go halfway up, which was a fair hike, and have good views over the water. You could even see all the way to Cooktown. You could just pick out the lighthouse and some of the houses and buildings that were white.

Cockatoo

Paster Medingdorfer with ploughing team, c. 1930

Bama who knew the Medingdorfers said they were kind-hearted and good to the people.

One of our favourite pastimes was climbing the gum trees near the church to play 'bear-bear'. You had to climb as high as you could to get away from the bear, or you would be grabbed. Smaller kids were often caught as they couldn't climb very high. The bigger kids climbed higher and some of them managed not to get caught.

We also played with tyres. These must have been from Muni's truck. Once, we pushed a tyre up the road and Mulun Darkan got into it. The tyre started rolling, not really fast but it was moving. Mulun's head must have been spinning! The tyre picked up speed, bouncing and spinning with Mulun inside. Eventually, the tyre rolled into a bit of a gully. We were a bit concerned about Mulun, but he jumped out laughing. We all burst out laughing then, it was such a funny sight.

There was also an old wheelbarrow wheel, attached to an axle that stuck out on both sides. I'd put my hands on the axle and content myself by pushing it along.

A wonderful time was the rainy season. We would go near the back of our house where there was a running stream. It was lovely clean water, very cool from the mountain. We also drank the water which was fresh and sweet. We had to be careful swimming when the stream was running fast, as it would push you downstream.

Cape Bedford did not have rich soil, but it was a beautiful area to live in. Muni thought of growing sisal hemp for export to Sydney, and tried to make the crop grow successfully but the soil was too

Dhabundhin

Dhabundhin was a natural leader and was in charge of Wayarego. When his brother, Harry Bungurr, was sent away, Dhabundhin pleaded with Muni for him not to go, but to no avail. He decided to go with him, and at Palm Island, Dhabundhin fulfilled his promise as a leader. He built the Anglican Church, and changed his name to Jack Dhabundhin. He was the son of Nhimanhlui, a Mangaar-warra man. Nhimanhlui was the sister of the famous mala-digarra brothers, Butchin and Gunguunbi.

Auntie Maudie was Dhabundhin's sweetheart. She was unable to go to Palm Island, and stayed behind to care for the dormitory girls. She was a strong influence in the community and never married.

Dhabundhin (centre back row)

Auntie Maudie Mulgal

Cockatoo

poor. Another idea was to make copra, as there were plenty of coconut palms planted by the first missionaries. Again, it was too hard to make a living. We used coconuts for eating and drinking the juice, and they were also used in cooking. Fish soup cooked with coconut provided a beautiful meal!

Muni had a garden with a cement well and some fruit trees, including mandarins. When the mandarins were in season, he picked them and put them into tea boxes. He called the children to his house and handed the mandarins out from those tea boxes. He also sometimes gave us lollies from town.

Wayarego supplied us with potatoes, pumpkins, sweet potatoes, and bananas. These were all brought across by whaleboat or mission boat. Muni also opened up land at Peter's Garden,

Muni growing sisal

The soil at Cape Bedford was poor, and the sisal crop was not successful for export.

Family life

Bêche-de-mer

north-west of Wayarego, to grow peanuts. This venture did not last long because it was hard to access the land.

As a young man, Uncle Harold had been sent to work at Wayarego. He looked after the horses and the ploughing. A lot of the men were working on the boats but my uncle was working the land. Uncle Harold was later sent to Palm Island where he became skilled with boats and won several races.

Most of the time our mothers were busy running the families because our fathers were away for long periods. They fished on boats for bêche-de-mer, trochus and dugong. We were often out with our mothers, fishing or swimming, and when our fathers were home we'd all be out together. I treasure my childhood memories of living at Hope Valley; it was such a good time of my life. I lived there until I was seven years old.

Cockatoo

Boats moored at Cooktown

Boats at Cape Bedford

European and Japanese fishermen used Aboriginal people to dive for pearl shell, trochus and bêche-de-mer in the Cooktown area throughout the nineteenth century. Men and women were exploited as forced labour, in conditions of extreme hardship and abuse. As a result of the deep water diving, most of these old bama men suffered from loss of hearing.

However, the Lutheran mission at Cape Bedford had its own boats and these were manned by bama. Under their Aboriginal captains, most famously George Bowen and Roy's father, Paddy McIvor, these boats plied the coast from the Hope Islands to Cape Bowen and Red Point. They collected trochus and bêche-de-mer for the overseas trade and dugong oil for export to other Aboriginal communities.

'Pearl Queen'

Dad was a leading seaman, and worked on the first mission boat, the 'Pearl Queen'. When the 'Ramona' was bought, he became the ship's captain, and had Mugay Woibo, Uncle Willie and others as his crew.

Chooks at sea

One day Dad had to sail the 'Pearl Queen' into Cooktown. Ngathi Karl wanted to come with him. There were a lot of fowls at the mission and they had a plan to sell some to the Chinese traders, once they got them past Muni. On the way, the wind blew up. As the boat heeled, the crates, which were stowed amidships, slipped. Sure enough, they ended up in the water. Luckily, the lids had come off and there were the chooks swimming around the boat! I don't know how many birds Dad, Ngathi Karl and the other boat crews managed to rescue, but we all laughed when we heard about it.

It must have been especially funny, because this was Ngathi Karl's first venture into the chookie business. As Karl was Dad's adoptive father-in-law, or ngathiina, Dad had to show some respect and restrain his laughter.

'Murrabal'
Barramundi, 2006

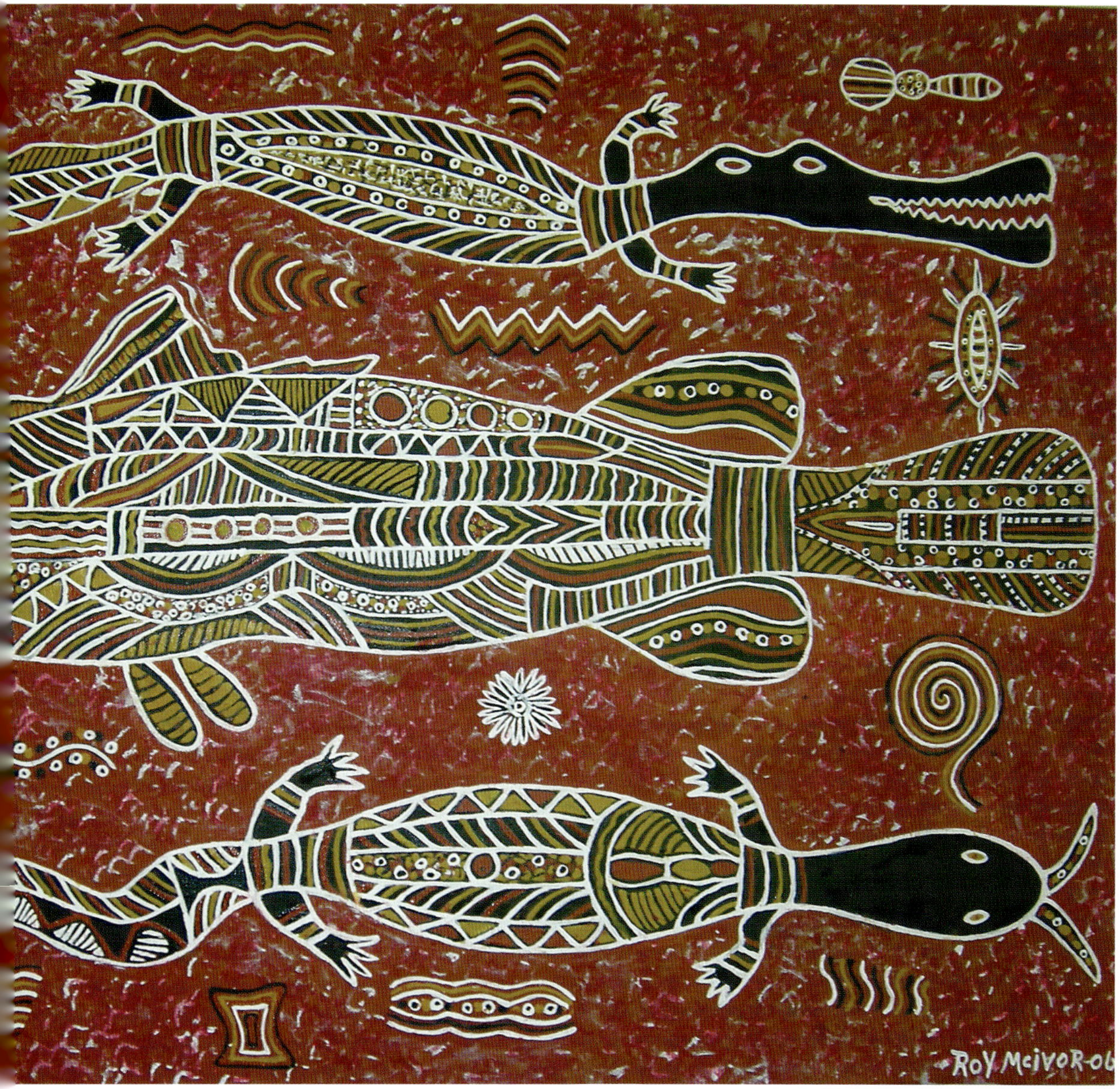
ROY McIVOR-06

Muni's residence and
garden at Eight Mile

CHAPTER THREE

Spring Hill

Muni had been looking around for better land to grow crops, and using his own funds he had negotiated with the church to buy land at Eight Mile and Spring Hill. In 1939, Muni told us we were going to set up a new mission at Spring Hill. Everyone from Hope Valley and from the outstations Elim, Wayarego and Ngaandalin were to live in Spring Hill together. The soil was better than at Cape Bedford, and this would help the mission to become more self-sufficient.

Muni and his wife would be stationed at Eight Mile with the single men. Mugay George Bowen, whose wife had recently passed away, was to live there as well with his sons Ted, Walter and Ernie. Victor Behrendorf, who had married Muni's daughter Grace Schwarz, was to be the caretaker at Spring Hill. He was from a well-known family in Biloela and was a great tradesman. He was our head builder and had trained many of our men.

Our fathers worked hard to set up the new mission. They built comfortable huts for each of the families, using bush timber. Alexander Palms were cut down and split. The harder outside wooden slats were used for the walls. Sometimes the men would

One of the cottages at Spring Hill

come home for a week or so, and then they'd go back to work. It was hard for the women, but the idea was that when Spring Hill and Eight Mile were set up, people would live there together.

We shifted to Spring Hill in 1940. We were among the first few to move. Auntie Dolly, Uncle Willie, my cousins, Mum, Dad, my siblings and I moved there in Muni's truck.

Driving in a truck for the first time was a strange experience — it appeared to me that the trees were running! Leo Rosendale was the driver. We went past Allen Point along the beach without any dramas. Deep Creek needed to be crossed with caution. There is the risk of bogging and losing your vehicle if it is crossed too slowly. Our driver was very skilled, and he crossed without any problems. We went along the beach and came to the turn-off to the Waandarin Gap. The truck had to climb up a steep road and it went along fine. Going along, there was another range before Bridge Creek. This is where the truck conked out. Leo Rosendale got under the hood and soon found the problem which he quickly fixed.

We continued our journey and came to Bridge Creek. This was a place where the old people, the traditional bama, lived

Bama with sweet potato crop

under the leadership of King Jacko of the Dyunydu clan. He was made king of the area around Bridge Creek, and lived in a camp on Reserve land, close to the mission, with his people and other non-Christian bama. They lived peacefully, working on the roads. They had previously worked on farms and used their skills to grow fruit and vegetables, including pawpaws, granadillas, jackfruit, cassava, corn, pumpkin and sweet potatoes. King Jacko had good relations with Muni, who relied on him to keep the roads in good order by laying corduroys over boggy patches, and to report any illegal activities to him. King Jacko's people were hard workers, and had cut saplings to place over the boggy patches.

We made it to Old Spring Hill, an outstation, without any further problems. Here we saw the station's house and gardens with crops of sweet potato and mango trees. Arthur, an old stockman lived there. We pulled up for a while and enjoyed a break before we headed off. We finally arrived at Spring Hill and a new chapter in our lives began. Other families that arrived soon after us were the Rosendales and Deerals.

The community was strong; it was teeming with life and great spirit. Young men like Peter Costello and Victor Cobus cleared parts of the forest, and planted watermelons in the log ash. Communal gardens were established, growing crops of sweet potatoes, cotton, oranges, bananas, pumpkins, peanuts, sweet corn, pawpaws, cassava, taro and melons. Some of the food was sold to the Chinese people in Cooktown, and Muni bought equipment to work the fields. Families also had their own scrub gardens. We had one, and Emily was encouraged to grow her own patch of peanuts.

Muni had purchased some hard-working horses from a man called Jack Brown. They were used for ploughing the fields, and I loved seeing the plough turn the soil. I remember smelling the horses' sweat from their hard work. It was great to see bama work together and plant things.

My life changed as I was now old enough to attend school. Our bush school building had not yet been completed, and the temporary school had bush leaves on the roof and blad
y grass on the walls. Ngathi Alick Cameron was our teacher, and old Arthur Phillip was the monitor. The students who started with me were my brother Syd, Pat Wallace, George Rosendale and his twin brothers Len and Lindsay, Eric and Henry Deeral. The girls did not go to school until the others arrived from the outstations.

Other buildings were constructed, including a beautiful church. Muni had ordered timbers from Cooktown. They were taken by boat to Fuller's Crossing, where a truck and a German wagon, towed by two horses, transported them to the church site. Dad, Uncle Willie, Mugay Woibo and Uncle Roy Dick worked on it with Mr Behrendorf. The church was officially opened on 30 June 1940. Two couples got married on that day. Roy Dick and Roger Hart married the Bowen sisters, May and Maudie. Years later I returned to Spring Hill to help break up the old church building. This was a sad occasion as it had fallen into disrepair. Soldiers had fired shots through the walls and broken the altar.

We had morning devotions at the church, held by Mr Behrendorf. Every family would be there. Muni held his services at Eight Mile. Sometimes he'd hold a Sunday service at Spring Hill, and the men from Eight Mile would walk over on those days. There was also a mid-weekly service. There were often games of German

Spring Hill

The new church at Spring Hill

football or cricket on Sundays, with the young men from Eight Mile divided into teams according to their binga thawuunh (traditional totem groups) — mirrgi (black bird) and wambal (carpenter bird).

At Spring Hill we had our own houses. We lived close to Aunty Dolly and Uncle Willie. The dwellings were comfortable and they stayed dry in the rain. It meant a great deal to us that they had been built by our fathers. They also built houses for the other families that were yet to arrive.

When the girls' dormitory was built, Emily and Gertie started going to school there with the girls from the outstations. Auntie Ann Cameron, Ngathi Alick and Auntie Maudie Mulgal were in charge of the girls. It was hard to get dress material for the girls, so some of them wore dresses made out of hessian bags. They must have been awfully itchy and hot during summer.

The boys' dormitory was built next, and we started going to school there. It was lovely to meet up with the boys from Cape Bedford, and to make friends with those from the outstations. There were a few fights, but they were always resolved peacefully. The fighters made friends again soon. The biblical saying 'Let not the sun go down upon your wrath' was imbedded in us.

Muni wanted to build a school, and preparations were made but the work was never finished. Muni had other ideas for buildings like a feeding place for mothers and children, where food would be distributed to families. There was also a building for packing cotton and distributing corn.

We loved to go to a beach called Gulnguy-guthar-bigu (place of old steamer wreck), on the North Shore facing Cooktown. To do so we had to climb over the range. We'd climb the hill, following a narrow road to get to the top from where you'd get a lovely view over Cooktown. The view here was much better than it was from Cape Bedford, which was too far away to see the houses properly. After catching our breath, we'd go down the other side of the hill to get to the beach. There was no scrub near the beach, but there was a patch of melons growing in a hollow. When they were ripe, we'd have a good feed which replenished our energy. Emily was stung by a box jellyfish at this beach. This was very serious as the sting can be lethal. She was in great pain, but she recovered.

We used to go to another place further down to get thuwan-ga (freshwater mussels), a great bush tucker. The women collected

Gulnguy-guthar-bigu

This is where the old steamer wreck lies, on the North Shore facing Cooktown. The view from here was much better than from Cape Bedford.

Spring Hill

'Gunhaar Gulithirr',
Angry crocodile,
c. 2005

Crocodile

I remember some ladies went swimming near a bend just up from Fuller's Crossing. The swimming hole was waist deep, and one of the ladies stood on something rough. She asked the others to feel what it was. They soon realised it was a crocodile. 'Walaa, ganhaarr! Look out, crocodile!' They all scrambled up the bank. Luckily, nobody got eaten!

them by gathering together in a circle in the fresh water. Cooked the right way, these mussels are a delicacy. They had to cook for a little more than an hour and then they could be eaten from the shell. They could also be taken out of the shell, chopped up finely and turned into a stew.

The ladies also collected thuwan-ga at Dulmba, just down from Fuller's Crossing. In those days there were fewer crocodiles about. Today it would be a dangerous place to swim but back then, people did. The women would come home with mussels and we just loved them. They were such good tucker.

Nineteen-forty-one was a great year. The families would go everywhere together. The men didn't have to leave for long periods, as nearly all the work was done in Spring Hill. Families grew their own fruit and vegetables. We even boiled sweet potato leaves, as well as leaves from another blue flower plant which Mum collected. There was also plenty of bush tucker around.

The mission had cattle and when a bullock was slaughtered, the meat was shared. When the men went hunting, they also shared their catch. On top of this, Muni still gave out rations.

The Angel

A mother was taken by a crocodile on the banks of the McIvor River. The mother and her daughter had gone fishing. The girl was only small, two or three years old. The mother must have been scaling fish at the water's edge, which might have attracted a crocodile with its gunabal (strong smell). The girl was playing on the sandbar, and did not see the attack. She arrived back at the camp by herself. When the old ladies asked her where her mother was, she said she was at the river, swimming.

'How did you get back here by yourself?' they asked. The child replied, 'I came with a lady in a long white dress.' 'Where is she now?' they asked. 'She's gone now,' replied the child. The old ladies agreed that it was an angel who had guided the child home to the camp.

When the bloodwood was in flower, there would be flying foxes around. My mother and I didn't like eating them, but they were considered a delicacy and many people loved them. We'd go out on moonlit nights and Dad, who was a skilled hunter, would spear them.

Dad was also good at spearing fish. He aimed the spear at the right part of the fish's body, where it would instantly kill it. It was good fishing off the rocks at Indian Head. If we were after murrabal (barramundi) and bigurrjirr (jewfish), we took our chances at Jepson's Crossing. The men would wade through the water, feeling on the leafy bottom with their feet for biguthirr. When they found one, they would spear it. At Thomas Creek there was a good spot to catch fresh water cod.

Hop trees grew at the back of our house. The branches grew thin and straight and Syd, Pat Wallace and I would cut them down and sharpen the ends for spears. We'd then cut down a zamia palm and roll this down a hill. As it was rolling, we'd spear it with our bush spears, trying to get it while it moved so fast. This was a lot of fun and we learnt how to spear. Once the stump was down the hill, we'd pull out our spears and push it uphill again.

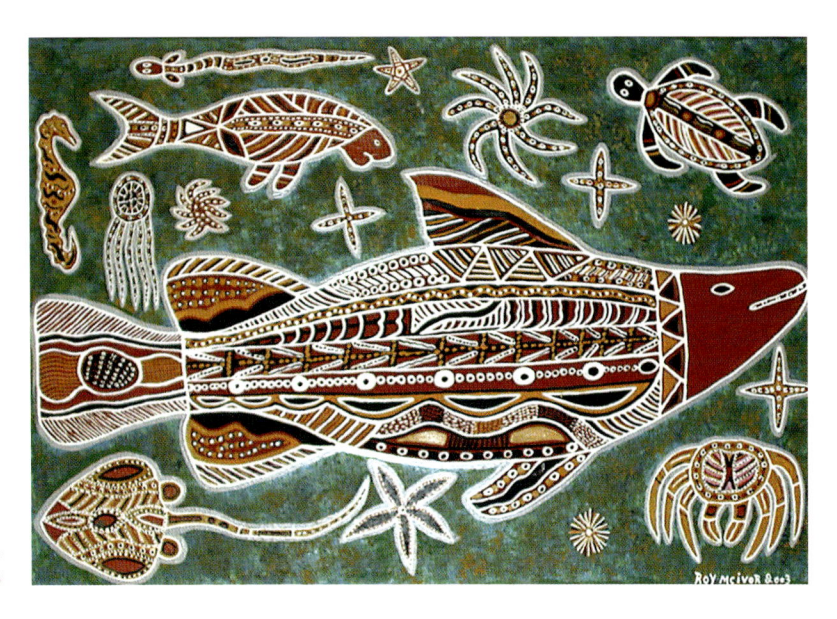

'Murrabal', Barramundi, 2003

Not far from home, there was a stream with a deep waterhole. We would go there after school, and one day I swam amongst the roots underneath the water. I had long curly hair, and it got entangled. Syd and my cousin saw I was in trouble and they jumped in and got me out. I don't think I'd be telling you this story today if I hadn't been rescued that day.

At times, we would cross the creek to gather bush foods from the sandhills. Tommy Convent, a Nugal man, looked after goats there and we had fun playing with them.

We also had dogs. One of them was Towser, an Alsatian. He was a good pig dog. Towser provided the community with a lot of pig meat. We also had a terrier called Guess, who was good at finding goannas, porcupines (echindna), turkeys and other animals. I recall a time when Dad and Ngathi Alick took the dogs Towser, Guess and Lassie to go hunting. A big brown snake came out from the grass and bit Ngathi Alick's dog, Lassie. It didn't take long for the dog to die, and Ngathi Alick cried and cried over that dog. He really loved his pets.

Bigibigi

One day, Dad took Syd and me to Eight Mile to camp. On our last day, we collected bamboo sticks for my father to use for making spears. Before we headed back, Tulo Gordon gave me a little bigibigi (pig) which he had found while he had been hunting.

I was really happy to look after it, and wanted to prove that I was strong enough to carry it home. My father told me, 'While you carry it, make sure you have the piglet's nose tucked in under your armpit. It will get used to you quickly that way.' I did just that, but the walk home was long and I soon got tired of carrying that little piggy, which seemed to get heavier with every step. Dad noticed I was struggling, and offered to carry it. I was happy to swap the pig for the bamboo as it was much lighter.

The pig became my best friend and it followed us everywhere. When we went to the swimming hole, it jumped in after us, even from the same height! Our little piggy became a very good swimmer. He camped near the shack, and sometimes he went missing but we always found him, foraging for food, digging up worms and roots. I dearly loved that little pig.

There came a time when Muni said to Dad, 'Well, Paddy, I might get you to go back to Hope Valley to check the place out.' The school was still standing together with some buildings which had to be knocked down, because the materials were needed for Spring Hill. Dad wanted to take the family. So we all got ready, with some food and bedding. Our cousins wanted to come with us, so Gertie, Pat and Lucy were included. When word got out to Gami Martha, Gami Emma and Nguuthurr Helena, they joined us as well.

We started early, walking along until we came to Brannigan's Crossing. Dad said we had to camp there. It was good to have a spell! I remember it was a lovely night, that camp by the creek's crossing. Mum cooked a couple of loaves of damper which we all enjoyed.

Dad woke us up the next morning and told us we had to get started as we had a long way to go. Instead of taking the road over the Waandarin Gap onto Alligator Beach, he decided to go to Elim. So that day we came to Buga Buluur Buluur, later called Triple B. That was Charlie McLean's place, where Herbert and Laura were born. Old Charlie McLean was pretty good at working up gardens. When we got there we found pineapples and paw paws. No-one lived there anymore, so we helped ourselves and had a bit of a spell.

Dad was following a road he remembered from old times. There was a track from Elim to Triple B, and another track from Elim through Bridge Creek to Spring Hill. Dad led us over the sandhills to Buurnga, a scrubby area thick with trees. Then we came to a waterhole. This waterhole, now hidden by swamp grasses, is near the road to Elim. I remember a plane flying overhead. I was so excited to see it that I dropped a billycan in the water. Dad tried to find it, but the water was too deep and it had gone right down to the bottom. Dad was not too impressed that I had lost a good billycan.

We got to the last gap in the ridge before Elim. Here you can see the beach and part of the bay in front of you, which is a beautiful sight. In the early 1950s, Charlie McLean, Mr Radke, his son Fred and others built the now existing road to Elim Beach. I think that

Cockatoo

Cape Bedford, taken from Elim

the road today still follows that old track. The part from where you have a beautiful view of the sea is near the waterhole where I dropped that billycan. The waterhole is covered up now and overgrown by bush. We went down to the flats where there is a swamp of pandanus palms. That night, we camped at the place where David Deemal lives today.

Before we settled for the night, we kids wanted to walk to the beach. The three old ladies took some fishing lines and went up the beach as well. They caught a good few fish, and then we heard them calling out, 'Walaa! Walaa! Yiki! Yiki! Look out! Ghosts!' They ran as fast as they could to the camp, and we wanted to know, 'What's wrong? What's wrong?' The ladies were terrified and puffing very hard, as they told us they had seen a thing like a great black bull coming towards them, trying to chase them.

Spring Hill

Sharing

According to the traditional ways of caring and sharing, you share some of what you get. In the old way, people would meet somewhere and camp together, and share their catch. We have the expressions walaan (good hunter) and matharr (incompetent and lazy). Back then, bama were proud to be called walaan, which is someone who shares and does things for others. Today you see more matharr – these are people who will take, but not share.

'Walaan gurra Matharr', Good hunters and lazy hunters, 2006

'It looks like a bull but we know it's a nguunha, a bad spirit, a ghost.' They brought back some lovely fish and Mum cooked them up in her boiler. We had a good meal, with enough fish for everyone and fish soup to drink as well.

Next morning we followed the beach to a place called Yargabadalbigu. The same place where Muni was met by the two warriors. We made our way to Hope Valley. It wasn't too far to walk and we got there by midday. The old school was still standing, and we made camp. We settled down on the verandah, and that night Dad and the old ladies told us stories. Later there was a ghostly presence and we could hear the sound of people crying. Dad heard footsteps coming up the steps, someone walking with boots on.

The next morning Dad said, 'I know who that fellow was, walking up the steps. He always wore boots. That was old Toby Summerhayse.' The butchers in Cooktown were called Summerhayse, and Toby worked in the slaughter-house for them until he came to Cape Bedford. He stayed at Hope Valley for a long time, and he died there. He was known as a relative of Mum and Aunty Dolly, as he came from Longreach. At the mission there was a shed with machines in it and Toby looked after them and camped there. One of the machines was a corn crusher. A lot of corn was brought to Hope Valley from the McIvor. It was crushed and made into cereal, which we used for breakfast with fresh cows' milk. Sometimes Mum would bake it, so it was useful to have that supply of cereal, crushed fine by the corn crusher.

The Devil and the Bible
Dad told me some yiki stories. In these stories, the yiki is the devil or the equivalent of Satan, the fallen angel. Some people have seen them.

Ngathi Karl was reading the Bible when an ugly yiki appeared. It was carrying a chain, as if ready to flog him. It yelled at him, 'Leave that book! Put it away! It's all lies! There's no such thing as it tells you... Give it up!' The old fellow refused to listen to him or obey. He had no intention of giving up his belief. When the yiki raised his chain to flog him, Ngathi Karl said the name of Jesus Christ and told him to leave him, to depart. And the yiki did go away.

Spring Hill

Early that morning, Dad went down to the well to get some of the sweet water. He saw somebody sitting on top of the cement work. This person was looking directly to the north. He turned round, looked at Dad and disappeared. Dad said he had no trouble in working out who he was. He came back with the billycan of water and said to us, 'You know what? I've just seen Ngathi Karl sitting down there at the well.'

Sometimes Aboriginal people see the spirit of a dead person. The name for this in Guugu Yimithirr is nguunha. Ngathi Karl had passed away at Cape Bedford. He had been like a grandfather to us and we knew he was fond of us kids.

After that, Dad checked the remaining houses and found most were in good order. It blew hard that day, and the old ladies took their lines and went fishing at the Breakwater. Again, they caught some nice fish. We were glad those three old ladies came along and provided us with fish on that trip!

The next day we started our walk home. We went along the beach, past Allen Point, and on to Thalgarr (Deep Creek). From there, we walked along to Waandarin Gap and through to Bridge Creek. This was the same road that we had taken in the truck when we left the old mission. From Bridge Creek, we went to Old Spring Hill outstation and then home. Dad had to wait for Muni to come to Spring Hill to give him his report on the houses.

One day, Bob Flinders and two other men went out in their dinghy to get some turtle. They caught two turtles, and sent out the message to everyone to come to the beach between Indian Head and Mt Saunders. This was a good lesson for us kids, to have those men sharing their meat.

Some of the dormitory boys, Tom (Mulli Mulli) and Toby Christie and Vernon and Robert Gordon, had been left behind and they started off later. They had to go through thick rainforest up the mountain. In the rainforest they saw creatures with black ugly bodies. There was a man, standing like an ape and he was looking east. There was a mother on the ground, with a little one at her breast and another little one standing beside her. They were half-human, half ape-like creatures. They were looking in the other direction and did not see the boys. The boys gestured to each other to go back. They slowly backed away before they turned around to gallop back to the dormitory. We call these creatures maargami-ngay, though the more common name is granhthin. They come on the wind and grab you when they can get a hold of you. If you are caught by them, you turn into one of them.

Once I was with Mugay George Bowen and some others on the Morgan River, near the junction of the Morgan and McIvor Rivers. We were sleeping in our swags under the stars when we heard a bellowing noise. We got some loose tea tree bark and lit a fire. The whirlwind creature veered away and went across the Morgan River to the old Ngaandalin mission. We could then hear it go through Gullal country and although it got that far

Maargami-ngay!

Dad went up to the Starcke River with some old people and some younger boys. They made a camp, and went off exploring. They followed the creek downstream and then saw a tree, shaking as though there was a big wind. On the back of this wind, the maargami came, and grabbed one of the boys. He screamed for help and the other boys ran back towards the camp. The old people started to shout, 'Maargami-ngay! Maargami-ngay! They are taking him up the mountain!' People could hear the boy's voice off in the distance as he was taken up the mountain and then over the ridges. The cheeky maargami were taking the boy around the mountains, away from them, and then closer again. They were teasing bama as if to say, 'We have one of yours, try to get it, I bet you can't!' The old people knew what to do. They took hold of a woomera and stood ready to grab the boy. When the maargami came nearer, they managed to wrestle him from the maargami's grasp.

But the boy had changed, and had turned into a maargami. He had sharp teeth and big floppy ears, and was black in colour. The old people built a fire and picked some broad leaves. They warmed them and placed them all over his body. They gave the boy a woomera to bite, and he held it between his sharp teeth. Slowly he came back to his human form.

Stories of the Maargami

There was a child who was left near a waterhole by her mother. Her mother could hear her daughter crying out and she could tell by the sound that the child had been changed into a maargami. The mother went to get help from an old man, who could turn the child back into a human being. He found the girl and gave her a milbirr (spear thrower) to bite. He used a wide, heart-shaped leaf from a small bush called thugulga (mango bark). He made a fire and warmed the leaf, which he then rubbed all over the girl's body. She became normal again.

away, we could still hear its horrible roaring noise. The noise was deafening, and I clearly remember the noise slowly carrying away in the distance. This was a manu-galga-thirr.

I remember another time when I was camping with Mugay George Bowen, Charlie Burns, and two or three other young men. Jacob Baru drove the army blitz truck to drop us off at the Muuwuntha waterholes on the McIvor River. We set up camp near the bora grounds and settled in for the night. Mugay George Bowen was the only one who used a sleeping bag. Between 9 and 10pm we were startled by a tremendous noise. It sounded like a cattle stampede was headed straight for us. We jumped up and climbed into the nearest trees. Mugay George Bowen was struggling with his sleeping bag and he could not get off the ground! Charlie Burns started singing out to us young fellas, 'Walaa, walaa! Someone help him. He will get trampled on. You can't just leave him lying there!' Nobody came forward and the noise travelled past us, though we could see nothing. This was not a stampede. It was a ghostly encounter.

On the other hand, dunggan are friendly spirits, who are light-hearted and playful. They enjoy swimming and diving for thuwanga. We have heard their shrill voices around the waterholes at Guuthi. Once I went to climb the Guuthi sandhill with Thelma and my sister, and we heard strange voices singing out. It sounded like the joyful shouts of children at play. I feel very fond of these harmless, captivating creatures and have portrayed them often in my paintings.

Cockatoo

Manu-galga-thirr

The manu-galga-thirr has more often been heard than seen, because of the loud noise it makes, which carries for miles. The creature is described as a dark being, which has sparks and flames coming off it. It has been seen eating the coals of dying fires, though it seems to be scared of bright light.

Yoren Walu Walu, a Yalmba-warra man, and Yimbatchi, a Thuubi-warra man, were travelling together. As it was getting late, they set up camp at Mahnbarr. They were using a bayan, a bark hut made with tea tree bark. The men awoke around midnight when a terrible noise startled them. They saw a creature approaching the camp, a dark figure with sparks flying from its body. Horrified, the men watched the creature as it stopped at the fire's embers and started eating the coals. They heard it making a sound like KKKRRRRR KKKRRRRR as it was feeding on the coals. Yoren wanted to bolt. Yimbatchi signalled to help him make a fire, while he whispered, 'It will scare him off.' The light of the fire did scare the creature. As it left, they could hear its terrible sound slowly fade in the far distance.

'Dunggangay Thawunhthirrgu', Friendly Spirit People, 2007

Dunggans are from the spirit world. They visit waterholes and lagoons, making merry, paddling canoes, laughing and screaming with joy and diving for fresh water mussels. Whenever people come nearby, talking or making any noise, the Dunggans disappear. Many of the Spirit beings are mischievous but Dunggans are special — they are friendly.

**'Manyjalbi Nanggurr',
Mountainside Camp, 2007**

Campsites were selected and then changed according to the needs of the time. Proximity to the water was important as well as access to the main source of available food. The menu of the month was dictated by which animals were fat. A protected cave made a good birthing place and site. It was often necessary to retreat to a mountainside camp during difficult weather.

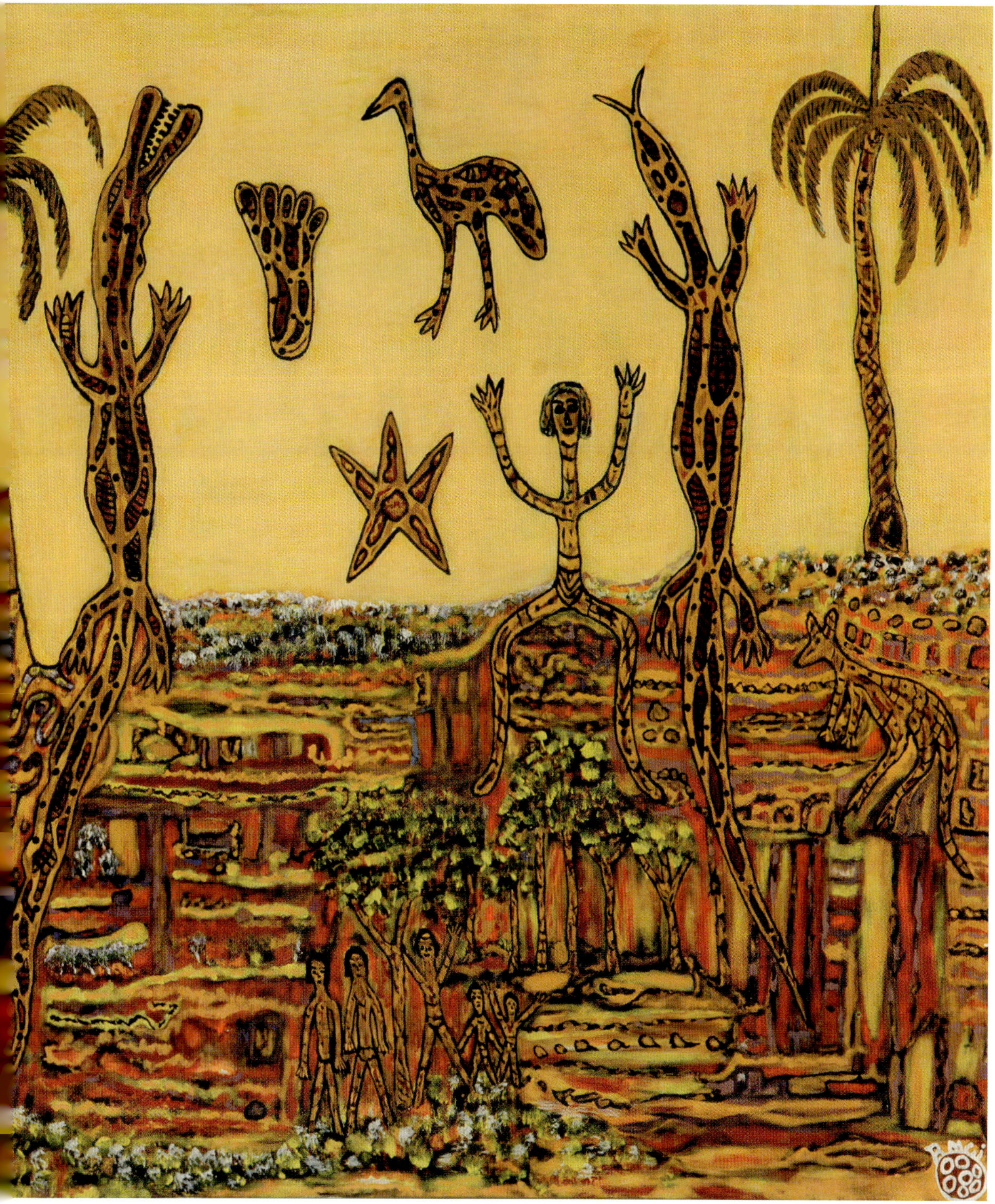

'Wungga baadildhil', Wailing Time, c. 2007

It was very sad to see our friends lying sick in the hospital wards. We lost a great number of our people at this time.

CHAPTER FOUR

Prisoners of war

Spring Hill was a happy time for me. We kids didn't know about violence, didn't know about hating anyone. Everybody minded their own business and we were all friends, and that is the way to be. But our lives were about to change again. Mr Behrendorf had an old gramophone, and he sometimes invited us over to listen to music on it at night. He also had a wireless. With that, we were able to gather news about the war with the Japanese.

The time came when we could no longer enjoy the gramophone, or listen to the radio. In 1942 Allied forces set up bases on Cape York, and they had an air strip at Four Mile. The war was getting worse, and Muni told us to leave the mission and move into safer inland hide-outs. Even though he hadn't been back to Germany for years, Muni was falsely accused of giving information to the enemy because of his nationality. There were also claims by the military that the Hope Valley bama were sending smoke signals or Morse code messages to help the Japanese. There was fear that our people might use their expertise to lead enemy troops through the bush. Some of the military even claimed that we spoke Japanese!

Cockatoo

The saltpans at Four Mile were used as an airstrip in the early days of the war, after the fall of Pearl Harbour, and before the Eight Mile airstrip had been started up. The area was low-lying and too small for some of the big planes, such as the Flying Fortress, which slid off the runway into the mud. This was an old ceremonial ground, used for the resolution of disputes. A former airman who came to Hope Vale as an electrician after the war told me that from a squadron of seventy men, only three remained.

The airstrip was busy, and we saw plenty of planes flying over and exercising. We would run out and wave at the pilots, but Muni told us to stop. He even suggested we hide in the cassava crop when the planes came overhead. Some of the planes that came back had smoke streaming from them, though we never heard what became of them and their pilots. Dad had a chisel and carpentry tools, and Syd, my cousin Pat and I started making models of the planes that we saw flying over. I developed my love for working with tools at that time.

When somebody spotted a washed-up mine on Gulnguy-guthar-bigu, we weren't allowed to go to that lovely beach anymore.

The McIvor, Wallace and Michael families had moved to an area of sand-ridges near Old Spring Hill. The men made good strong humpies, and we were comfortable living there, but the war intensified, and we were told to move again. All the families made humpies along the right branch of the Endeavour River. Dad built us a shack near Fuller's Crossing, and Uncle Willie's family was just across the river. The Pearsons were down from us and others were further away. School had stopped and it was a lonely time as we never got to see the other kids. They seemed to have disappeared. There were times when we'd walk back to our scrub gardens, looking for vegetables. Piggy always came on these walks. We also had chooks, and we would knock one over every now and then, to have something to eat.

Dad hunted with my mother and they would bring home goannas, bandicoots and porcupine. The other men were good hunters too, and would go out with Dad and Towser. I remember going out with Dad one day, and Towser spotted a diwaan (scrub turkey) up in a tree. I didn't think Dad would be able to hit it, but he proved again what a great hunter he was when he speared that turkey with great accuracy.

Families still gathered for Sunday services. They were held at the shed which was used for the dormitory girls' hide-out. Mr Fuller had built this shed at Fuller's Crossing. We used to need a dinghy to cross this part of the river, but now Mr Behrendorf had built a swinging bridge across it. It really swayed!

We had to cross the bridge to get our rations, and one time I remember we were just about to cross when a huge, heavy plane flew over really low. It made the leaves of the trees tremble and the ground shook. We were later told it was an American bomber, on its way to Darwin.

One day, Syd, Pat and I were sitting on the riverbank playing with a butcher's knife, having fun digging holes in the sand. We glanced up and saw Aunty Dolly send our little cousin Harold across the river, carrying porridge in a pot. We saw him get onto the log to cross over the deep water. Aunty must have had her eye on him, too. Next thing, he slipped and fell into the water. Aunty was off in a flash, running onto the log and jumping into the water to pull him out. She was quick! Of course, Harold lost the pot of porridge.

Aunty came up to us, growling, 'Why didn't you run to rescue him?' We didn't reply, as it was clear she had outrun us. We couldn't have beaten her to it. She gave us a good growling anyway. When Harold came to our camp empty-handed, Mum got worked up about it too.

Precious things

When I returned after the war to help dismantle the church at Spring Hill, I found my way back to our old shelter on the sand-ridge. My father had stored many of our precious possessions here. Most of the books and papers had decayed, but I found Dad's telescope from the Ramona, an old coconut grater, a sieve and the family Bible, still in good condition.

Cockatoo

Allegations

Although the Protector and the Department of Aboriginal Affairs had known for months about the Hope Valley relocation, no planning or provision of decent services was organised. To this day, this war crime has never been trialled, and it is not clear why the Hope Valley people were moved. Some thought it was because of their allegiance to Muni, while others believe it was because of rumours that the Hope Valley bama were communicating with the Japanese through morse code and smoke signals. There is also speculation that it may have been because the military wanted to move their landing strip from Four Mile to the more strategic site of Muni's land at Eight Mile. The military did this only a few months after the Hope Valley people were taken away.

My life took an unexpected turn when the mission community was suddenly exiled to a government settlement at Woorabinda in Central Queensland. Woorabinda had been established in the 1920s as a reserve for Aboriginal people from throughout the state who had been forcibly removed and placed there under the control of the government.

It was 17 May 1942, my sister Emily's birthday. That day we walked up with Mum and Dad to Spring Hill to get a couple of fowls. Dad killed them and they were cooking in the boiler with some pumpkins and other vegetables from the garden. We were sitting around on logs, about to be served with this big stew, when we heard people coming through the scrub. When Dad saw they were wearing uniforms, he knew they must be soldiers or policemen. They came up to the camp, stood there and asked what we were doing. Dad explained that it was his daughter's birthday and that we were about to have a birthday celebration meal.

To our surprise, they responded by saying, 'No. Leave that. Leave everything here.' So we never ate that wonderful stew. 'Come on, get up,' they said. 'It's time to move. Leave everything.' We had no choice. There was clothing and bedding nearby, but they refused to let us take it. 'Leave everything,' they said.

We came to Jepson's Crossing and there was a truck, the last one, as the other families had already left. The final two families to leave were the McIvors and Wallaces, along with Gami Martha, Gami Emma and Nguuthurr Helena. The soldiers told us to be quiet and to sit down in the truck. We were worried about Towser and my little piggy. It was so hard to leave them. I still remember my little pig standing there as we drove off.

We were driven to Eight Mile where Muni had a plantation of fruit trees, with bananas, oranges and mandarins. Some soldiers jumped off the truck and picked oranges for us kids. Before the truck started off again, a soldier said to my sister Ruth, 'What a beautiful girl you are, with curly hair. I think you may end up in Hollywood one day.' Later, in Woorabinda when the picture-shows came to town, my mind went back to that day and I remembered hearing about Hollywood for the first time.

As we crossed the main bridge over the Endeavour River, we saw Hubert Barry, an Aboriginal fellow from Cooktown, sitting there waving to us. Hubert, his wife and their children, stayed in Cooktown during the war. As we drove along, we passed the old airstrip at Four Mile. It was full of war planes. I remembered watching the planes taking off and landing, sometimes smoking or in flames, from Spring Hill.

At last we stopped at Number Three Wharf in Cooktown. Only the last piles of it are standing today. There used to be a big shed nearby, which is where we camped that night. There was nothing provided for us, not even toilets. We were hungry; we had not eaten anything all day apart from the fruit from Muni's plantation. We did not get a feed that night either. We spent an uncomfortable

Number Three Wharf, Cooktown, c. 1933

Only the last piles of it are standing today.

Cockatoo

Bama at waiting on the wharf, Cooktown, 1942

There were soldiers on either side, with guns. It was like herding a mob of cattle.

night sleeping on a cold dirt floor. We had only the clothes we stood up in, children and babies were crying, and our parents were anxious and apprehensive. No-one knew where we were going or what to expect. Were we prisoners of war? Were we being sent away because Muni was German and our people were suspected of helping the Japanese? Were we going to be sent to prison?

My thoughts kept going back to that lovely pot of stew we'd missed out on. I think some of the boys from the dormitory at Eight Mile had it in mind to swim across the channel to North Shore and get back to Eight Mile, but that didn't happen.

We were woken by the whistle of the big steamer 'Poonbar' as she came alongside. We were lined up and sent up the gangplank. Towser must have followed us. He was sitting, looking up at us as we boarded. Dad tried to walk down to shoo him away but a soldier ordered him to get up onto the deck. That was our last sight of Towser. Royce Lee took care of some of our dogs, but I never found out what happened to Towser.

Intelligence information

Years later, I was working in the orange plantation at Woorabinda when I saw a motor-car arrive. Dad told me the visitor was an ex-military Australian policeman who had been in Cooktown at the time of our removal from Spring Hill. He told my Dad that what the military had in mind was to flog and drag the Aboriginal people and Muni through the streets of Cooktown to teach them a lesson.

Prisoners of war

Detail from the Milbi Wall at Cooktown, showing the 'Poonbar', that took us from Cooktown to Cairns in 1942

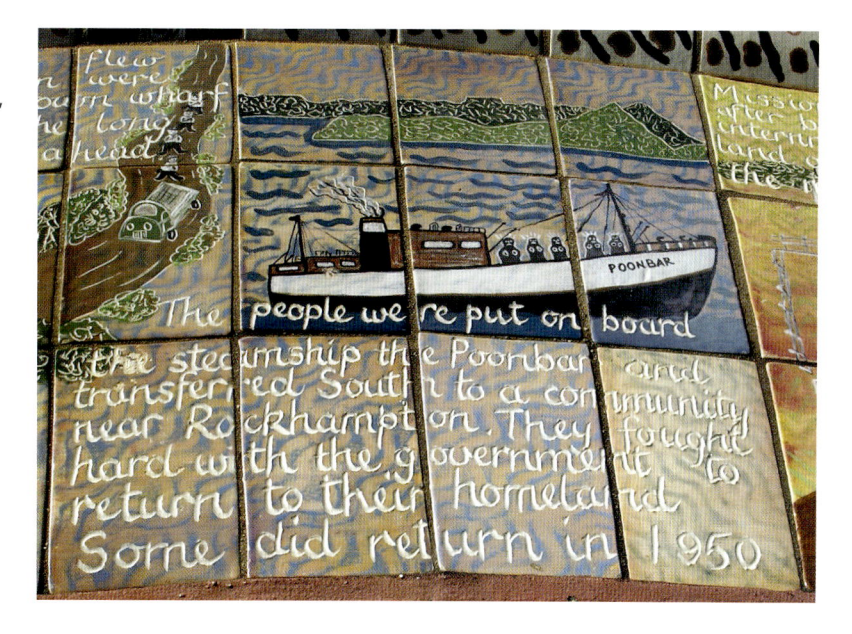

When everybody was on board, the whistle blew and the ship moved slowly from the wharf, out to the open sea. It was pretty rough that day. A lot of people were seasick. We had all been given Weetbix to eat, and people began vomiting over the rails. We didn't know if it was because the milk may have been sour, but the journey seemed very long. Somewhere along the way, the ship let off steam. It came with a burst of smoke, and everyone panicked. Uncle Roy Dick was ready to jump over the side, but Dad managed to hold him back. The captain tried to reassure us, and called Muni, who was aboard in a separate area. Muni spoke in Guugu Yimithirr to calm us down, 'Ganaa yurra-ngay murrga steam diigaay. It is alright, the boat is only letting off steam.'

Late in the evening, after journeying for about twelve hours, we arrived in Cairns. It had been a slow boat to China. We were very thirsty after that long trip. There had been no water for us to drink while we were on board. At about 7pm we boarded a train. We had never seen anything like it. The kids thought we had got into a house, and then the house started moving! People were hungry and dehydrated. We were given nothing to eat. When we stopped in Cardwell, some of the men got off to collect fruit. We went on through the night and the next day stopped in

Maudie Mulgal and Gami Emma

The final families to leave were the McIvors and Wallaces, along with Gami Martha, Gami Emma and Nguuthurr Helena. The soldiers told us to be quiet and to sit down in the truck.

Townsville. There was a meal served in the railway refreshment rooms there. We were starved after not having eaten for three days, and welcomed the meal wholeheartedly.

When the food was finished, Mr Foote, the Superintendent of Palm Island, came and told us he would take the old people to Palm Island. There were more tears and distress at this announcement. We had to say goodbye as the old people were taken to the bus, which took them to the jetty and the boat.

We said our goodbyes to Gami Emma, Gami Martha, Nguuthurr Helena and her son Freddy Capebedford, William Daku, and Tommy Convent, his wife Lena and their children Frank, Timmy and Lizzie. Gami Emma eventually returned to Hope Vale, but Gami Martha and Nguuthurr Helena both died on Palm Island.

We had to board another train heading for Mackay. Here the Lutheran Mission Guild came to the railway refreshment rooms with sandwiches and tea. We travelled on to Rockhampton and then on to Baralaba. It was freezing cold, but there was hot water boiling for tea in boilers over a log fire. Trucks came from Baralaba and Woorabinda. It took several truck-loads to shift everyone. After warming up a little at the fire with some tea, we got onto the truck around 7pm for the last freezing-cold leg of our journey to Woorabinda.

Prisoners of war

The Hope Valley community at Woorabinda

For two weeks, we slept on the bare floor of the freezing school buildings.

It was school holidays when we finally ended our journey and arrived at Woorabinda. We were exhausted and fearful, and preparations were in chaos. There was no welcome hot meal, and we waited a long time before we got that hot meal. Although Woorabinda was in a frost-belt, we were told to sleep on the cold floor of the empty school building. No blankets, no mattresses and no warm clothes. This was our first night in what, unbeknown to us, was to be our home for the next eight years. We didn't find out till much later that Muni had been interned at a POW camp in Brisbane.

There was no housing organised before our arrival, although some of the people at Woorabinda offered to share their houses with a few of our families. During this time, the superintendent, Mr Colledge, asked my father to organise the men into cutting saplings and stringy bark to make bark bush huts with a dirt floor. There were wagons, drays and draft horses available and the men were issued with axes and cross-cut saws. They went out into the bush and cut poles and stringy bark and the huts were gradually built. They built bark huts and the families were happier now that they had a place to stay.

Cockatoo

Funeral services
While Muni was imprisoned, Dad took on the spiritual leadership for our people. He conducted services every Sunday and Wednesday. He also conducted our people's funeral services, and made the coffins. The old horse Trooper was busy pulling coffins to the cemetery. One coffin after the other went there. These were such sad times.

It wasn't long before our people began to get sick. The first death occurred within a few days when Henry Baru's sister, Rita, passed away. Most children were healthy, and at first it was the younger ones who died. Then some of the older girls got sick. Later, it was boys in their teens. It was very sad to see our friends in the hospital. We lost a great number of our people at this time.

Emily became sick at the same time as my mother. Mum had recently given birth to my youngest sister, Kathleen. Mum recovered, but Emily was in hospital for a long time. She was finally so weak that the matron sent her home. Emily died in 1943 at the age of thirteen. It was a real blow. She was such a bright, clever girl, maybe the cleverest in the family. She was a loving sister and we dearly missed her.

There was an incident which occurred before Emily got sick when she was on the front verandah of our hut with Mum, Dorothy, Ruth and Kathleen. Above them, the sky was clear. There was rain out west, with distant thunder. Both front and back doors of the house were open. Suddenly a ball of lightning appeared and passed through the front door, down the passageway, and out the back door! Nothing was burnt or harmed in any way.

Emily saw the heavens open when she was dying. She exclaimed, 'Look at the bright light! I can see Ngathi Karl, and there are many others with him. He has people following him, lots of followers!' Dad made her coffin and a wooden cross. With a hot wire, Dad carved her name and memorial words on a wooden plaque that he had made. Dad also conducted her funeral. When I returned to Woorabinda more than forty years later, Emily's cross was the only one left standing. The others had rotted away.

I was sent to the Woorabinda hospital two or three times but managed to get better. The doctor was an Australian army doctor and he couldn't identify my illness. Anyway, there were few medicines available. There were many people hospitalised, and the doctor only called in weekly. He was given the nickname Dr Alright as he assured his patients that they would be alright. Staff weren't sure what diseases they were dealing with, and the medicines they had did not cure the patients. Major Mango, a Nugal-warra bama, lost three of his children in one day.

Herbert McLean, a friend of mine who was only ten at the time, remembers being in hospital with a carbuncle on his shoulder. He was there when two men in his ward died, not long after they had beeen treated. Herbert was terrified and was bawling his eyes out when his father walked in. His dad was very angry, and he stormed out and rushed over to the Superintendent's office.

When Mum was ill, she would not go to sleep until the early hours of the morning. Mum was in the women's ward where a number of young girls died. She said that the matron did late rounds with a torch checking who was asleep. When the matron shone the torch on Mum and saw that she was awake, she walked on.

Another epidemic started, and this time we got the measles. In the hot weather we were very uncomfortable. Our house was one of six built on blocks. It wasn't very high but we were able to creep under and sleep where it was cooler. I can't remember how long we were sick for, but it made us very miserable! It is a disease that comes once in a lifetime. I never had measles again.

Our people are dying

The effect of the exile on our people was devastating. We arrived at Woorabinda strong and healthy. Of the 235 people exiled, a third died, many of them children. Every Hope Valley family was touched by this tragedy.

Suspicions arose about the medical treatment we were receiving. These rumours have persisted and many troubling questions remain unanswered. Why did the Department of Native Affairs move us? Why was Woorabinda so ill-prepared for our arrival? Why were there so many deaths among our people while the Woorabinda people remained relatively healthy?

**'Wawungan',
Spirit realm, 2001**

I entered this painting in the Laura Art Award of 2003 and won first prize. In this painting, traditional symbols are depicted in an abstract form. This is an important painting to me as I see in it some of the abstract qualities I developed in my later work.

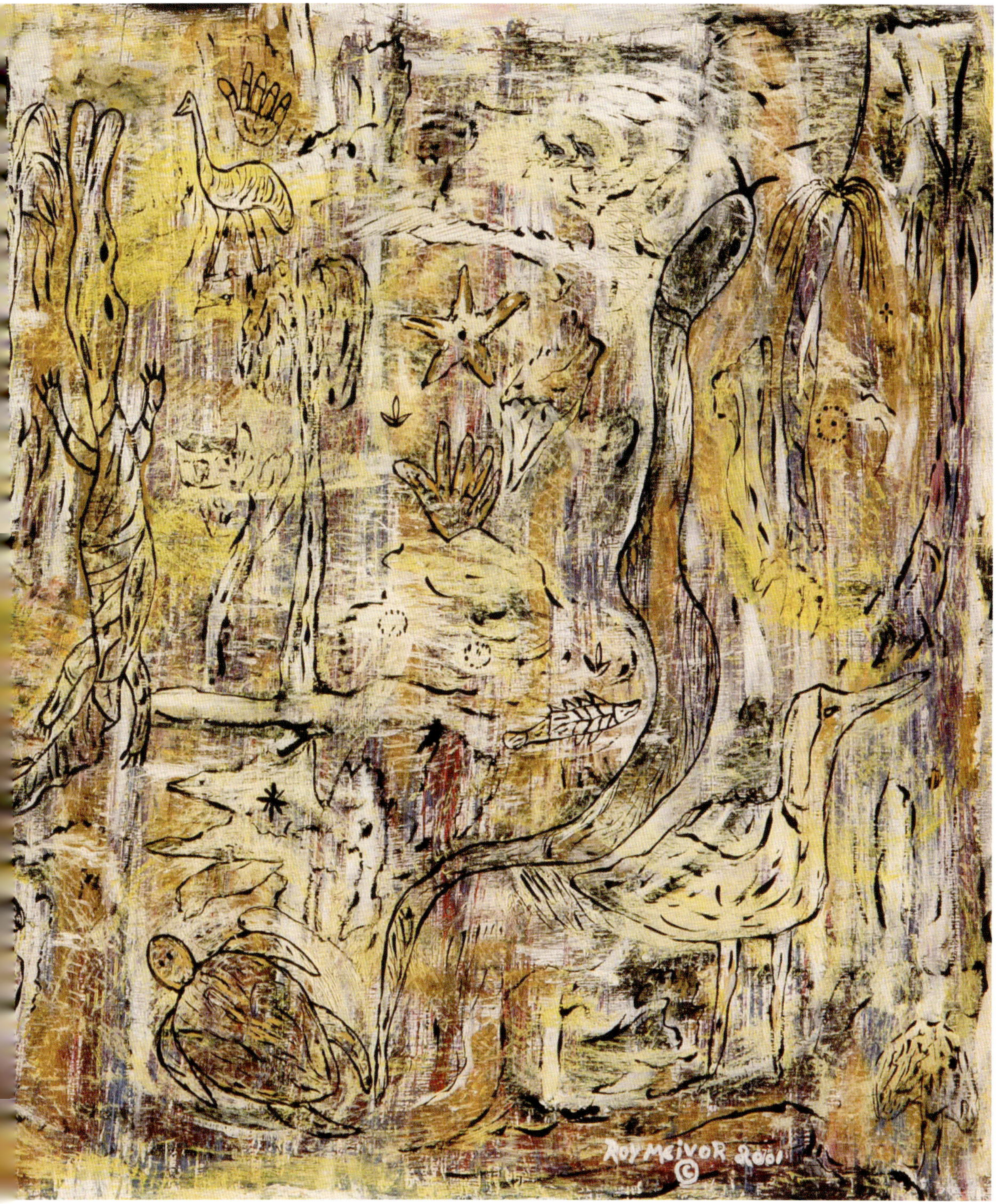
ROY McIVOR 2001 ©

'Ngalburrin',
Imprisoned, 2006

CHAPTER FIVE

Years of exile

Not long after we had settled into our hut, a lady came along and Mum was talking to her. Mum said, 'See the lady over there?' while she pointed towards my auntie. 'That is my sister. We come from Stonehenge, just out from Longreach.' The lady reacted with surprise, 'What? You are from Stonehenge? You are my people! My people are from there, you know!' The word spread quickly and others came around who were also from out west. Mum's cousin also came and introduced herself.

Mum met a lot of her people in this time. She also tried hard to trace her older brother, Uncle Henry, but she never managed to find him. She sent him letters, but they all got sent back. Both Auntie Dolly and Mum were very disappointed that they never managed to find him again. Years later we found out that Uncle Henry had been educated and brought up by white people and was granted an 'exemption from the Act' in 1916, when he was twenty years old. I now think that he may have joined the army and served in WWI as we have found no trace of him.

One time, while we were still staying at the school, our mothers thought it a good idea to take us children for a walk. We walked

Cockatoo

towards a big building which blocked the scene behind it. When we got past the building, we saw people dressed up in costumes, painted up, preparing for a corroboree. We had never seen these costumes before. Once the kids stopped being scared, they thought it was interesting to watch! There were different dance groups and Mum recognised one group from Stonehenge. They had bush leaves on small branches tied up near their knees. The dancers were all painted up.

I used to watch the performances with Eric Deeral, Henry Baru and other friends. The men would cut down hollow logs, light fires at their base and stand them up to throw a light on the scene. One night there was a man from the Tablelands, Dick Douglas from Malanda, who was a relative of Fred Deeral and Dick Gordonvale. I think Eric called him grandfather. Well, this

'Yimbaala', Corroboree, 2007

Some kids were really scared. They were clinging onto their mothers' dresses and they tried to hide behind their mothers' skirts, screaming, 'Yiki yiki!' Our mothers said, 'No, this is a corroboree, you know, shake a leg.'

fellow performed the possum dance. He had cut down a tree, not a really large one, and they had stripped it of leaves. He climbed the tree and acted like a possum. I clearly remember one of his performances. That night, he got right up the tree, acting out his possum ritual. He must have slipped because the next minute he was down on the ground. Ruby Flinders called out, 'Yurrangay nganthangun gulaan bulii bubuwii! Look at that possum; he fell on the ground!' He was not hurt too badly, and we all had a good laugh.

There were many corroborees, and there was this particular one which was acted out really slowly, in slow motion. It was performed by an old man, Bunda. He may have been from Bundaberg, but I'm not sure. It was a thrill for us one night when men from Barrow Point and Bathurst Bay danced traditional malkari (corroboree).

The time came for us to start school. School began with preparatory grades 1–4, and then primary grades 1–4. Our first teacher was Mr Tarlington, a lay minister for the Church of England at Woorabinda. At times we got caned on the legs, and sometimes he swiped us on the hands. He'd then get us to turn our hands over and hit us on the knuckles. It was awful on a cold day. Woorabinda was a cold place. The taps used to freeze overnight. People collected water in buckets from communal taps, and on cold days we had to wait till the sun was shining before we could get some water.

Mr Tarlington stayed for a couple of years, and then Mr Fritz arrived from Thursday Island. He used to call students out to the front and make them wear a dunce's cap. Henry Baru was called out and made to stand on a desk at the back of the classroom, wearing a dunce's cap. Mr Fritz mocked him and said, 'Everyone, turn around and look at Papa, the sailor-man.' It was embarrassing and a bad thing to do, but we could do nothing to stop it.

Mr Fritz was a good artist. He painted the 'Wandana', a ship that used to call in at Cooktown. He had two daughters who used to come to school. They did not mix with us, and sat on

Cockatoo

Henry Baru

The late Henry Baru, Roy's best friend, had sharper memories of these fights than Roy: Because we Hope Valley mission Bama had been evacuated and our German missionary interned, we were teased by the other children at Woorabinda. They would give the Nazi salute and shout 'Heil Hitler!' at us, or they would call us 'mission monkeys' who had been sent from the bush with no clothes on. We boys would push Roy McIvor to the front to defend our honour. Roy was a keen defender.

---

the verandah to do their work. The other teachers were the head teacher and his wife, who was second in charge. There were also some Aboriginal monitors who helped teach the kids. Some of these were really good. They never hit us.

The boys' dormitory was used for Sunday and mid-weekly services. Sometimes the Anglican Church and the Inland Mission sent us an invitation to attend a service. We had our own Sunday school, with our elder Ngathi Alick Cameron in charge. Ngathi Alick later became an ordained pastor.

We often went to the Baptist Church, where we learnt a few of the choruses, singing along with the congregation. They also handed out tickets for having learnt Bible verses. Now and then they used to have examinations, and if you were very good you could win a six-star award. It was a top award and my sister Emily won it. She was given a framed biblical picture, and we were all very proud of her.

We boys from the north loved playing round the village and along the banks of the Mimosa River. Eight Mile was an easy walk from the settlement, and had a rocky pool with cool water. We'd wander around with our bows and arrows and shanghais, and occasionally we knocked down a bird. Sometimes we met up with Woorabinda kids, and there would be a fight on. Generally, we were good friends. There were some fights: these were usually resolved, but sometimes they weren't.

Years of exile

We also got into mischief. There was a quiet heifer which we boys were keen to ride. One day we went to find it, and found it feeding quietly in a gorge. We bailed it up, and were ready to jump on its back, when next thing we heard a whip-crack and some shouting. Oscar Munns, the head stockman and his men had spotted us! We were set to receive a good growling. We ran for it, but as I ran I stepped on a sharp stick, which bounced up and got me on the side of the knee. I still have the scar today; it is the shape of a boomerang. Blood was pouring all over my leg. I was in pain and ready to faint. Oscar Munns caught up with me and ended up taking me to the hospital on his buckboard. There I was in the hospital. I had been given a good bath and I was lying in bed, dressed in pyjamas. Someone had given me a drink and my dizziness had gone away. Next to me, in the drawer of my bedside table, I had managed to hide my shanghai and some of the stones that I had carried in my pocket!

I remember cutting a sapling and threading it with twine to make a play horse. On the banks of the Mimosa we played the game of bear-bear as we had at Cape Bedford. Charlie McLean had the idea of making an area for the Hope Valley children to use as a playground. Mr Colledge, the superintendent, agreed and an area was set aside for games. Sometimes the Woorabinda kids would join us.

At Woorabinda, there was a curfew and you had to be home by 9pm. There was a rostered policeman on patrol and if you were caught, there was trouble. At the police station, there were three well-lit jail houses at the front and one dark cell in the back. If you

Dad's school book

Dad often spoke about being aware of the consequences of our actions. He used different stories as teaching tools, but the idea was the same. Like a boomerang, your bad actions will come back to hurt you. I remember one of these stories. Out west, there were three Aboriginal stockmen mustering. One evening, they were riding home towards sunset. There was lightning in the western sky. The rider in the middle of the three began to swear and curse God. Suddenly, he was struck by lightning. Nothing was left but his charred remains. The other two men saw this as punishment for his impiety.

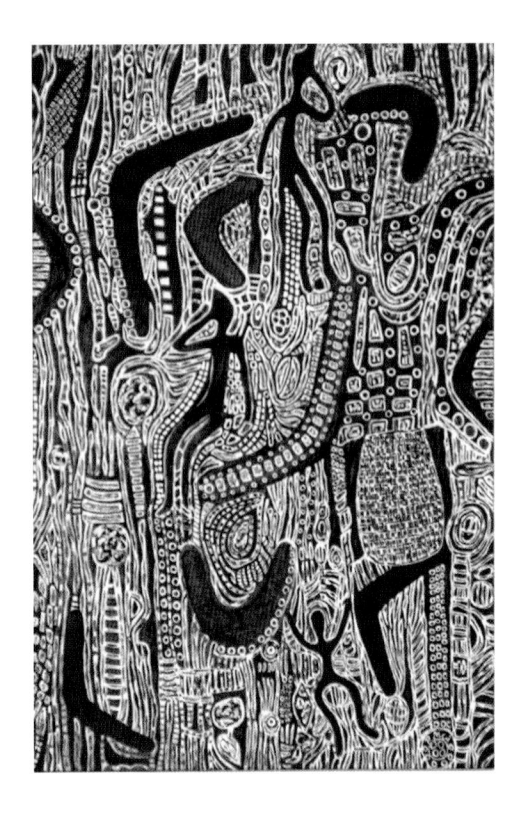

'Warraygurr-gurra Warmbaaya', Whatever you give out comes back twofold, 2007

were caught doing something wrong, you would be put in the back cell for twenty-one days and not let out. It was a dark, black cell.

One evening, when Eric and I went to watch a corroboree, I got into a fight with a Woorabinda boy. Soon after the fight broke out, a policeman arrived and blew his whistle. Other policemen arrived and took us to the police station. The sergeant, who knew us well, assessed the situation. He told me to go home and the other boy was locked in jail for the night.

One day, George Rosendale, Pat Wallace, Barney Major and I went cycling along on Perch Creek Road. On our way back from our ride, we saw a crowd had gathered near the river and we knew something had happened. Someone said, 'A fella has drowned here, Walla Wilson.' Walla was from Palm Island. He had been a great dancer, and everyone enjoyed watching him perform his Island Dance. He was also a great footballer and boxer. One time, Walla spent twenty-one days in jail after he had a fight with some of the boys from Woorabinda. Poor Walla had to spend all of those days in that dark cell and when he came out he had a long beard.

They reckoned that he had swum from Possum Island, where he was detained at an earlier time, to Palm Island! He had done so to escape, and succeeded. We thought it was suspicious that he had managed to swim such a long distance, yet drowned in the Mimosa River just after the floods. Some people had seen him wave his hand while he was drowning. Ted Bowen was the one who found him. They had to wait for the water to go down before the body could be taken out. There was a huge burial for him, as he had been very popular. He was sadly missed.

Our parents knew where we were and we were given a lot of independence, which we did not abuse. We used to walk in the brigalow bush and pick blackberries, sweet fruit a bit like bunday in the north. There was another very tasty fruit called wild mango, a bit like our dharbun. One day a group of older boys, Lex Deemal, Pat Wallace, and Archie Gibson were in the bush, trying to frighten us — Henry Baru, Eric Deeral, Ted Barney and I. The older boys were howling like dingoes. We ran away in fright, jumping over logs. Henry crashed into a fallen wattle tree. He caught his foot and fell headlong onto the ground. We tried to stifle our laughter till we saw Henry was laughing as well.

Old Harry Green carted firewood, and we'd run alongside his dray with our hessian bags. He let us hop on and took us out to the boxwood trees where we could collect firewood. His traditional land was in Brisbane at a place called Indooroopilly, which means 'a place of many waterholes'. In later years when I was in Brisbane with Henry Baru, working in the Indooroopilly area, I often thought of the old fellow. He was so kind, helping the families out with firewood. He lived alone in the bush.

One day we kids went out to his place and we couldn't work out how he got water, as there was no creek. He kept dingo pups at his house. We used to walk past it on our way to 'Niagara Falls', which was a beautiful waterfall with clear water to swim in. There we'd wander round, watching the birds as they swooped down to drink from the waterhole. The big buck kangaroos used to leap high when they were disturbed.

On weekends we went hunting kangaroos. There were lots of kangaroos around Woorabinda. The name comes from the words woora (kangaroo) and binda (sit down). These kangaroos were huge. They were so good to watch racing away, lifting up their tails and powering off. At a safe distance, they'd stop and watch you. We'd have our minds set to kill one for bush tucker, which would be a great change from the beef we so often ate. Their meat was used to make pies which were sold in the community.

We also used to go looking for goannas at Eight Mile. The goannas dug holes in the bank, and we went out looking for their tails. When you spotted a tail, you quickly pulled the goanna from its hole and broke its neck. Porcupine was another animal we hunted. The porcupine is considered a delicacy as its meat is tender. We also enjoyed going down the river and watching the Hereford cattle. At times, we were lucky enough to catch a bull fight. When this happened, we always climbed a tree to watch the fight from a safe distance.

There didn't seem to be a wet season at Woorabinda. When we had rain, it came from the west, instead of the east, and that would get the river running. Vegetables grew well and there were citrus fruits, even grapes and peaches. Watermelons and mulberries grew in abundance.

We had many forms of entertainment. Sometimes there were English dances and we'd go there to watch. There were good mouth organ and accordion players who played the music. The men dressed up and the ladies wore pretty long dresses. It was a joy to watch them.

Boxing was on Saturday afternoons, and was very popular. There were good fighters from Woorabinda and Palm Island. I only saw one from Cherbourg, David Twaddle, a really good boxer. Sometimes the young boys used to fight in the boxing ring, but it never got out of control. There always was a good referee. George, one of the Sibley brothers from Palm Island, was the champion fighter. Some of our men like Bedford and Stanley Darkan, Phillip Wallace, and Walter and Bindi Jack were also good. Bindi Jack and Phillip Wallace later became Australian champions. Other boxers were Michael Charlie, Ernie McGreen (a good left-hander) and Archie Gibson. My brother and I wanted to box, and there was an old trainer named Billy Rooked who gave tough training lessons. We were going to start training with him, but then we left Woorabinda.

There was also a football team. Every Sunday afternoon there'd be a football match in Biloela, Rockhampton, Mt Morgan, Clermont, Theodore and other places. The first match we went to at Woorabinda was a good one, but towards the end a couple of the Woorabinda fellows, Steven Saunders and Reggie Richardson, got into a fight. Both men had blood on their faces. Nobody interrupted them, they just let the strongest one win. I don't know who won actually — they both looked pretty bloody at the end of it! We were very shocked by this. We had watched games up in the north and they had never ended in a fight.

Rodeo

A rodeo was held annually in Baralaba, and the Woorabinda trucks would take us there. We saw riders from cattle stations near and far.

The Woorabinda players were well-trained. However, they had a hard time playing the team from Mt Morgan, which was made up of miners. These players were tough and they mostly beat Woorabinda. Cherbourg put up a good game as well.

At the Baralaba rodeo we saw riders from cattle stations near and far. The three best riders were brothers, George, Jack and Wally Hayden. George and Jack put up a good show riding together back to front and they would stick on. Wally was an expert at buck-jump riding.

During the rodeo there was always a show where people brought artefacts to display and sell. School children made things like axe-handles, pencil cases, inkwells and suitcases, and prizes were awarded for the displays.

There was also a picture-theatre nearby in Baralaba, where we could watch war-time movies with stars like Ava Gardner, Judy Garland Rock Hudson and Van Johnston. I remember watching many movies, including Bette Davis in 'Sing Me the Song of the Island' and Elizabeth Taylor in 'Lassie Come Home'.

At the time we weren't allowed to get secondary education. We were taught the basics and the final level of education wouldn't have been higher than Grade 4. Mr Jarrett noticed that his pupils were eager to learn more, and so he taught us extra. He opened the school at night for further education classes, teaching maths and other subjects to adults and young people who had already left school. People really appreciated that. Everybody enjoyed his teaching. There were a lot of clever kids around. One bright student was Paul Burns, from Palm Island. He was so bright that he was allowed secondary education. He went to Mt Carmel in Charters Towers and ended up working as a clerk in the Department of Native Affairs in Cairns.

We were also taught skills like cabinet making, metalwork and tin-smithing. There was a stringy bark tree which people used for building houses, and there was another type we called ringie stringy. We looked for dead ringie stringy which we chopped down and split. Then we polished the wood; it could be made into a walking stick. It looked like a snake as it curved and had lovely markings. Dad was an expert at making beautifully carved walking sticks.

When he wasn't working away, Mugay George Bowen, who was gifted in woodwork and using the lathe, taught us how to make suitcases of plywood, axe handles of blue gum, and inkwell stands of ringie stringy. Later on, Mugay George made statues of Captain Cook and they looked so real it was incredible! He also produced gunstocks from mango tree branches and walking sticks, as did my father and Uncle Roy Dick.

Mrs Jarrett was our art teacher. She gave us lessons when Mr Jarrett was busy teaching the older children. We had to colour our drawings with pastels. I loved to do this, and my feelings for art must have begun at this time. When the time came for me to leave school, Mrs Jarrett said she hoped I would continue with my art. Her words were a great inspiration. She also taught the girls to crochet, and my sister Dorothy still loves to crochet. Whenever there was a show at Woorabinda, our work was on display. People would come from Baralaba, Duaringa, Rockhampton and the surrounding stations to buy the work and people got money from the sales.

Dad

The authorities at Woorabinda relied so heavily on Dad that he was not allowed to work outside the community. Superintendent Mr Colledge trusted him as a spokesperson for our people. When electricity was installed at the settlement, a Mr Hoffmann, who had worked on the construction of the Panama Canal, was in charge of setting up a pump to bring water from the swamp in order to generate electricity. He asked Dad to make up the boxing for the motors and turbines which were housed near the cement works by the lagoon. Dad completed the job and received the highest compliments from Hoffman, who said the work was spot-on!

Cockatoo

Bama at Pimpama

New experiences
During their exile, bama from Hope Valley had to adapt to an unknown way of life. Many had not even experienced Cooktown. The men who went to work on outstations and elsewhere as part of the war effort received wages for the first time. Most men travelled in a variety of jobs, learning new skills and meeting new people. To the credit of their strength of character and faith, they survived the traumas as stronger people.

In September 1942, a party of Woorabinda men together with Uncle Willie, Harry Costello, Bartie Deemal and Frank and Tim Convent were sent to the Atherton Tablelands. They were the first group sent out to work as part of the war effort. They spent a few months there, and were then sent to other places mainly in South Queensland. While the men were away, they could not attend the funerals of some of their loved ones.

Mugay Woibo and Uncle Willie were often in charge of the working parties who went out to the cotton farms at Biloela, peanut farms at Kingaroy, and cane farms at Bundaberg. The women were left behind to manage the families. It must have been hard for our mothers, with the men away, just as they had been at Hope Valley working out on the boats.

Indigenous soldiers

During both World Wars, many Aboriginal men volunteered for service overseas, and others joined the Volunteer Defence Corps for service within Australia. During WWI, recruitment officers visited the mission at Cape Bedford. They tried to recruit Dad and others, but Muni managed to intervene. However, during their exile in Woorabinda, the Hope Valley men were involved in the war effort. They went to work on farms all round south-east Queensland, and Indigenous men joined up for training and service. Many men received greater pay and social contacts than they had experienced before. Their contribution to the war effort, however, has remained unacknowledged.

Some of the men cutting cane at Bundaberg bought bicycles, which were called Bundy Star. While they were away, we used to ride them. Syd and I made good use of Dad's bike. We loved riding the bikes, and stayed on them till after dark.

Syd went to Pimpama, south of Brisbane, with some young men from Woorabinda and Cape Bedford. They were cutting bananas and sending them down a steep slope by flying fox. One of the Barnes boys got onto the flying fox and came hurtling down. They thought he would be killed, but he landed safely. After Syd came home, he got a job out west on a cattle station.

In 1944, Muni was released from his internment, and Leo Rosendale, his faithful driver, went to pick him up. We kids went out along the road to look for them. We climbed some trees and were sitting in the branches when we saw the truck coming along with Muni in it. We all sang out, 'Muni! Muni!' And he waved to us as they passed. The next day, in Woorabinda, one of the local men cursed Muni and swore at him. Although he was a young man and in good health, that man died the following day. This made a big impression on us!

Cockatoo

Peter Gibson and his family lived next door to us. George Gibson had bought a good bike, which Doug Gibson used. One Saturday, I slipped out of the house before morning devotions and Doug and I went riding. We raced down the road but I ran into a sandy patch. My front wheel twisted sideways and I flew off. My left arm went through the front wheel spokes and I heard a crack, while I felt a terrible pain. Doug came running and helped me get my arm out of the spokes. He could see my arm wasn't right. I couldn't ride home so I had to walk, holding my arm. When I got near the house, Mum saw me and she came out and gave me a good growling. Not only had I missed morning devotions, but she had wanted me to do some jobs. Anyway, I ended up in the Woorabinda hospital. I was in pain, because there weren't enough painkillers to go around.

It wasn't until Monday that I was put on a truck to Duaringa, where I caught the train to Rockhampton. There were a couple of people who had to make sure I would get there without any problems. The train left the station that evening, and we arrived a few hours later. I was operated on, and my arm was set. Coming out of the operation, I was in terrible pain. I had to stay in the hospital for a long time and while I was there, I caught a bug. The hospital superintendent sent the message to Dad that I was very ill and he came to visit me. I was happy to see him, but after two or three days when he said he was leaving, I pleaded with him to stay. I clung to him, crying, 'Don't leave, don't leave, Dad!' I was very sad to see him walk away.

I was slowly getting better and was allowed to walk around the hospital. It was still wartime and the hospital was busy, bringing in wounded troops. Sometimes I'd see the ambulance calling in with wounded men. There would be Americans, Australians and even Canadians. Sitting on the verandah, I could enjoy the view of the warplanes flying in from the Coral Sea. It was good to watch the planes fly in formation, probably over Yeppoon. I also saw American bombers, which made a terrible noise. When they flew over the hospital, the noise almost shook the building. They would fly to Sydney and further on from there.

The airstrip at Rockhampton was busy. I remember an American plane crashed on the Rocky airstrip. About eleven of the crew were treated for shock. Their beds were all around me, and they were very talkative. Many of the troops took pity on me and gave me some shillings. I ended up getting a lot of coins from those soldiers! Some of the American soldiers said they flew to Sydney, then on to Darwin and other places.

When Dad came again, he stayed at his carpenter friend's place. This man, Reggie Dodd, was a Palm Islander whom we met at Woorabinda. He had moved to Rockhampton with his family. His son Ralph was my friend, and we went to school together.

I caught a bus to visit my father one day, but Reggie's wife told me Dad had gone up the main street, towards the Post Office. I walked up, dodging the busy military traffic. There were heaps of American troops, and I saw a big brawl. American Military Police came in on their bikes to stop the fight. You usually heard about Australian soldiers fighting American soldiers, but this time the Americans were fighting each other.

From a distance, I saw three people sitting at the steps of the Post Office and I could work out that one of them was Dad. George Gibson and Bedford Darkan were with him. They had come in from one of the cattle stations, further north from Rocky. After a while we walked to the shops, where we bought sandwiches and drinks. We sat down under a tree to have our food. A rodeo was on and we decided to go and see it. This was the famous Rocky Roundup. I didn't see any bull-riding, but there was steer-riding and buck-jumping. Again, one of those famous cattlemen, the Hayden brothers, came first.

When I was about to be discharged, Dad came to pick me up. We took the train from Rocky via Mt Morgan to Baralaba, where we met up with the Ramus family. Noel Ramus was my best mate at the time. The Woorabinda truck came to Baralaba to pick up food for the store, and we caught a ride back on it. Before we left, Noel told me he had heard that Mr Jarrett had left the school, and that we had a new teacher. We got back home on the weekend, so it wasn't until I went back to school that I discovered that Noel had been wrong. To my great relief, Mr Jarrett was still there.

Cockatoo

I had been away for a long time, and I had put on a lot of weight. I went swimming and walking around and played games with my mates. Soon my body was back to normal. We used to meet at the sports ground set up by Charlie McLean.

Not long after that, Charlie got a job at Oaks Station, and the whole family moved. I lost the company of my good mate Herbert for a year or so. His mother had died while we were still living at Cape Bedford, and Charlie was looking after the kids. Herbert's sister Laura was my cousin Gertie's best friend. Herbert lost a year or two of school, but he managed to catch up when he came back. We were reaching the age when we thought we were now men, and we wore long trousers. However, when we approached the teacher to see if we could leave school, he said that we were still too young. We could leave at sixteen, almost two years away.

When my classmates and I finally finished school, it was a major life-change. We felt a mixture of fear and excitement at the prospect of starting work. We received our grown-up government issue: khaki shirts and shorts, Blucher boots and a felt hat. In my first job, Eric Deeral and I worked as offsiders on the 'ghost truck', a white truck driven by Ian Murphy. We were carting sand for cement work. Then Eric left to work on a cattle station at Raby Creek.

Ted Barney and I got a job cutting firewood for the girls' dormitory and when this was finished, we did it for one of the staff homes. I soon got bored and I began farm work with the men, clearing weeds in the citrus plantation. Next, I worked with Dad and Jellicoe Jacko as a builder's mate. Jellicoe had been crew on the Ramona when Dad was the captain.

I applied for a job at Foleyvale Station where I was paid £2.10. This meant I could give some to my mother to add to her child endowment allowance. For the first time mothers had started to receive child endowment. I was sad to leave, but I rolled my swag and got on the truck to Duaringa. Foleyvale was divided into a top and a bottom camp. At first, we bunked in a big tent at the top camp. Between both camps ran the McKenzie River, which we had to cross. The manager was Mr McCann. He and his family had a lovely house. The farm was worked by Woorabinda and Cape Bedford men.

Foleyvale was on country rich in black soil. It was good for growing sorghum, and got very boggy after the rain. Oscar Munns, the Woorabinda stockman, would come out for branding and mustering. It was also good cattle country, typical of that Capricornia area around Rockhampton. There was thick brigalow scrub with many diwaan and goannas. Sometimes we would find these goannas in hollow logs and spy them out with a mirror. They were big enough to be frightening. There were also wungguurrga (plains turkeys) on the farmland, and they would be shot and cooked up.

In flood-time the bridges over the McKenzie River would go under, and the men from Cape Bedford used a four-paddle dinghy to get the men across to the bottom camp.

Joe Malcolm and I had to shift camp and go to work at the bottom stock camp with Les Airey and Billy Rollston, two Woorabinda men. In this camp, we had a very good cook who made beautiful scones and stews. Two of the men there were excellent horsemen. Les Airey was a champion buck-jump rider. He used to ride at the Woorabinda show and he never fell off. Our job was to get the draft horses, harness them to the wagon and go to the Six Mile waterhole to collect water. We had to fill five or six 44-gallon drums and take water to the camp. We tried swimming in the waterhole, and there were freshwater turtles, almost as big as

One night, Billy Rollston was late coming back to the camp. 9 o'clock came and then it was past 10. At the camp there was a bough shelter made up from cut branches, to give shade. The boss, Mr McCann, took Joe and me in his jeep out to the boundary fence of the neighbouring station to look for Bill. We were singing out, but there was no sign of him. We went back to camp and Mr McCann said he'd burn the bough shelter as a signal. He lit it and when it was in flames, old Billy appeared. He was very angry. 'What's the idea of burning that bough shed? Don't you know I'm an old bushman and I never get lost?'

small sea turtles. Joe and I had other work to do with the men, clearing logs. During this time we got used to handling horses. The draft horses were strong pulling horses, and we soon enjoyed working with them.

One day, Les asked me to get the cows from the bottom of the hollow. I had to ride Sunny, who was an ambler, with a hard mouth. I couldn't ride and the horse must have known this because he bolted down into the hollow. He took off over fallen logs, heading for the saddling paddock, while I clung on.

Another time, I went to get the cows on a big horse, a galloper. After I'd got the cows into the yard, he bolted. The men at the stock camp saw me galloping, and said to themselves, 'That Roy, he's a quick learner!' There was a line of barbed wire leading from a tree to the stock camp and we were heading towards it. I thought I was going to be cut in half, and I surely would have died, but the horse propped to a standstill just in time, and I stuck on.

There was another incident, this time on a quiet horse. We were going up a steep slope and the saddle slid off. I came off with it, sliding over the horse's rump. These incidents did not deter me from learning about horses and becoming a good rider. In fact, in those days I felt a strong desire to become a great stockman. I made up my mind that I would go out west when the job at Foleyvale came to an end.

It was good to be out in the bush and working with men from Woorabinda and our home country. Our community leaders operated in the same way as they had at Cape Bedford among the boatmen, the stockmen and farmworkers at the outstations. Billy Jacko was the elder at top Foleyvale, taking devotions night and morning and leading the singing from the Sankey and the Lutheran hymn books. Major Mango was in charge at the bottom camp. The shifts lasted a fortnight and men were collected from camps on a Friday, received their pay, and returned to work the following Monday.

Bush camp stories

We had some good times there. One evening, two Woorabinda men came to the stock camp and asked Bill if they could camp with us as it was getting late. However, there was no room so I agreed to walk with them to a gate on the way back to their camp about a mile away. One of them was laughing to himself, and then the other man disappeared. I got suspicious and I asked where he'd gone. The fellow just told me to keep going. We got to the gate, which had a big tree next to it and the fellow with me started to laugh. I turned around and out from behind the tree came this ghostly figure, the other man draped in a sheet. I was terrified and the two of them were laughing at the fun.

'Ganhaarr', Crocodile, 2005

**'Birra gurra walngangay',
Homeland river lagoon, 2006**

In my country there is a significant river, the McIvor River, and creeks and lagoons feed into. Water means life in the land and it supports many other life forms – eels, fish, lily pods, ducks, geese, pigeons and all kinds of other birds and animals. Lagoons were the refrigerator of the past, a thamaan – a place of plenty.

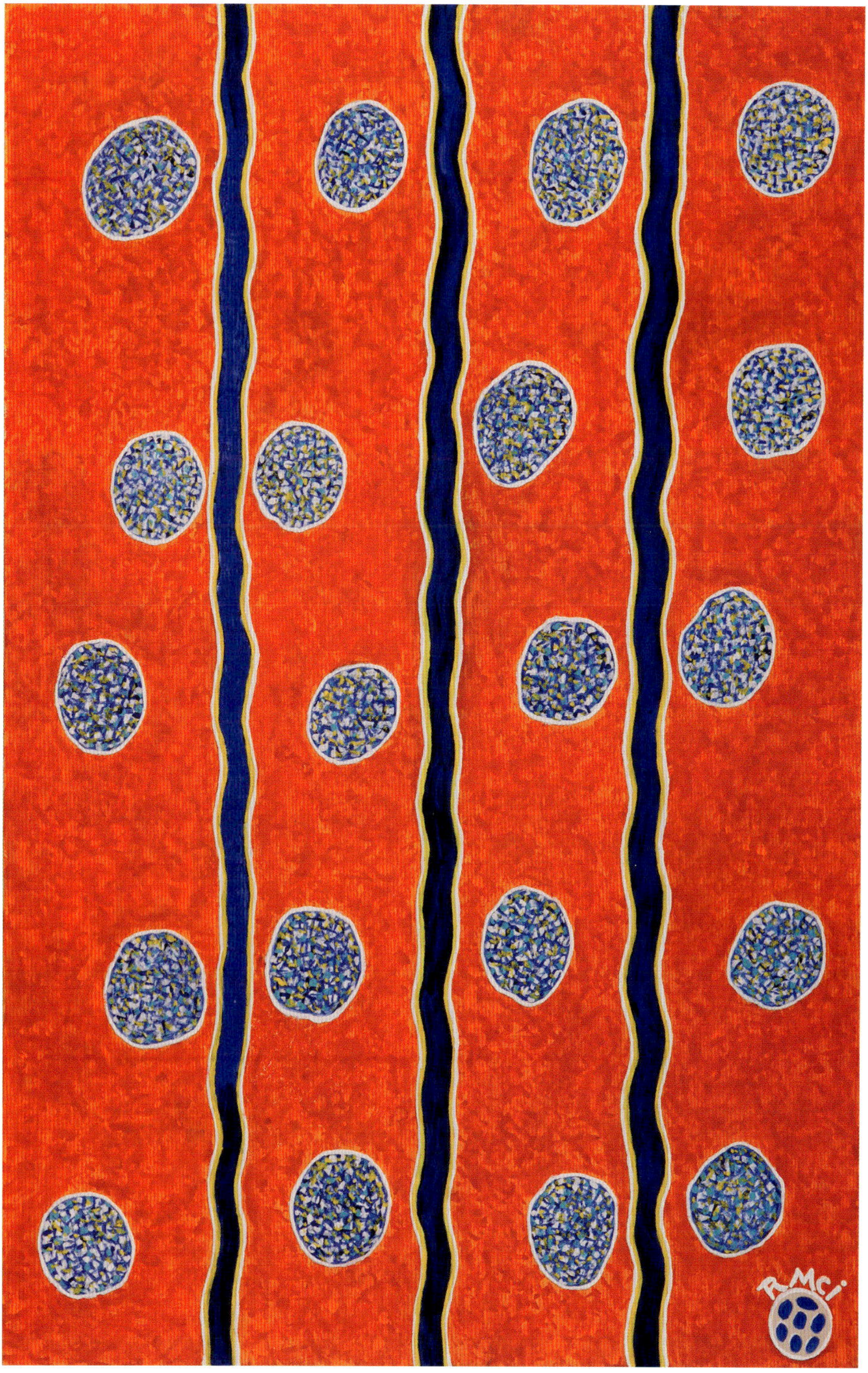
R.Mci

Early pioneers leaving Woorabinda

All through that year, there were groups of men returning. These early groups were called the pioneers.

CHAPTER SIX

My people want to go home

My father always worked in the best interests of the Hope Valley bama, and without his leadership, there would be no Hope Vale today. After the war and the dreadful loss of our bama, our elders grew restless in the desire to return to the north. Even though Mum and Auntie had relatives there, they did not feel at home at Woorabinda. Dad and the other elders, Mugay George Bowen and Ngathi Alick Cameron, kept up the pressure on the church and government authorities to return the Guugu Yimithirr people to the north. 'Guwaar thatanu. Let us go home', was a commonly heard cry.

My parents were offered a chance to re-settle in Rockhampton and 'exemption from the Act', but without hesitation, they chose to return to their home-country.

With the help of the church, Dad, Ngathi Alick Cameron and Mugay George Bowen went to Brisbane to meet with Joh Bjelke Peterson, who was a Member of Parliament and a Lutheran. They discussed their intentions with Joh, who was sympathetic to their cause. With his support, they finally got the long-awaited answer that they could go home. Their persistence won out and

Cockatoo

Meeting Joh Bjelke-Petersen at St Peters Lutheran College. Left to right: George Bowen, Joh Bjelke Petersen, Frank Behrendorf, Pastor Vic Wenke and Paddy McIvor

a new mission in the north was planned at Hope Vale. Dad and other elders then went as delegates to Lutheran congregations in Bundaberg, Mackay and other places to appeal for funds to make the return home possible.

In early 1949, Dad and Syd were called to go north with the third group of men, together with Herman Radke and his son Fred, to help set up the new mission. All through that year, there were groups of men returning. These early groups were called the pioneers. The first lot of eight men dismantled the army buildings at Eight Mile. These materials were used for the first houses. The Woorabinda people didn't understand that we wanted to leave, and begged their friends to stay. But our old people were determined to return to their country.

In February 1950, word came for my family that we were to leave Woorabinda and journey north. We were to go with the wives and children of Uncle Willie, Uncle Roy Dick, Billy McGreen,

Jellicoe Jacko and Ted Bowen. We were the first group of women, children and adolescents to leave the south to meet up with the husbands and fathers at the new mission at Hope Vale. Our Woorabinda friends were amazed at our determination. They hadn't believed we would go.

I gave up my desire to go west and work as a stockman, as my mother and sisters needed my help with the move. There was a big truck to take the families from Woorabinda. We made it over the Duaringa Range, but the creek near Cooma Balaroo Station was overflowing. The manager of the station came to the crossing and saw what was happening. Our truck driver asked the station manager to get help. After some time, Barclay's carrier came out with an ex-serviceman who had served in New Guinea, six tea chests and a tarpaulin. The chests were wrapped in the tarpaulin and this structure was tightly bound together by ropes. On this construction we floated the kids, the luggage and even some of the ladies. We all got safely across and caught the train from Duaringa that night. It was just as well I was there with the twins, Leonard and Lindsay Rosendale, to help the women with the luggage and manage the kids. The ladies were very thankful to have us with them.

I can't remember much about the trip from Duaringa to Cairns. Frank Behrendorf met us in Cairns and took us out to Parramatta Park where we spent the night. The next day we caught the weekly Hayles boat, either the Merinda or the Malanda. It was a good trip, not rough. On the boat with us was a man called Charlie Tayley who, I later found out, had kinship links with both Guugu Yimithirr and Kuku Yalanji. No-one talked to him, but he must have understood all the chatter amongst the ladies. We arrived in Cooktown around 3 o'clock. No-one was there to meet us. The wet season had begun, and the creeks were flooding. We slept in Donald and Black's old store, near what is now the old Westpac bank building in Cooktown.

In the morning we found that the bridge over the Endeavour River was flooded and so we went by rail-motor as far as the siding at Wilton. There we were met by Mr Jones, an old drover who lived alone at a place near Endeavour Falls. He had come across to help us out. We had to cross the Endeavour River near Mt Olive Station to get onto the road to Hope Vale. Leonard, Lindsay, the older children and I waded across the river, and three or four of the ladies rode across on horses. This was the first time I saw Mum on a horse but unfortunately, no-one had a camera! After this ordeal, and carrying our baggage, we were relieved to see the big red mission truck with Leo Rosendale and Monty Woibo, ready to pick us up. Everyone was very happy to get onto the mission truck. We all knew Leo was a good driver.

Without any further dramas, we arrived at Hope Vale. The pioneers had been waiting eagerly for our arrival, and it was a great reunion. We had a good meal at the cookhouse near the boys' dormitory. Uncle Willie was in charge of the cookhouse. We were surprised to see what those first men had achieved in such a short time! There were already houses set up for the pastor, the staff, the schoolteachers, carpenters. There was even a store. There were vegetable gardens with pawpaws, sweet potatoes, corn, pumpkin, taro and bananas. Corn was growing in the open areas. Men were working with cattle.

My first job was land clearing. Then I joined Dad and Syd building. Our group was made up of David Deemal (my brother-in-law), Jellicoe Jacko, Harry Costello and Uncle Roy Dick. Eddie Bowen and Barnie McGreen joined a bit later. We worked in two gangs. The first priority was to establish the saw mill. A saw bench was set up and a few logs were cut. Ted Bowen was in charge. The eight families there were living in military huts which had been brought from Eight Mile, and set up on newly-cut stumps.

We dismantled the boys' dormitory at Eight Mile. The materials were used for several buildings in Hope Vale: the church manse, the old school, the boys' and girls' dormitories and the old hospital. The timbers were stacked in piles in front of where our church is today. While he was unravelling the timbers, George Rosendale was bitten by a taipan. He got very ill and was hospitalised for a long time. He spent a few weeks going in and out of a coma but survived the ordeal.

The first school class held at Hope Vale

We continued to build. The staff quarters and tin shacks for temporary housing were built in quick succession. We proceeded with building cottages for the families after the temporary living arrangements were finished.

Clarrie Hartwig was the building overseer. He wanted a team of men to build the school, and chose Dad, Syd, Jellicoe and me. It was measured out and the stumps were cut from boxwood, brought in by a tractor pulling a sledge. Crosscut saws were used to cut logs for the mill and stumps for the buildings. Within a week the stumps were set up. Some timber came from Eight Mile. The bottom plates were put in, then the weatherboard sides. Finally, we put on the iron roof. The building had one big room and a verandah. More families returned from the south and the children started going to school. Both my sisters were in that first group. Church services were held there.

Our first pastor was Vic Wenke, who arrived in 1950. He had served as a pastor in Biloela, and used to come to Woorabinda every month. Our teacher was Miss Haebich, from Guluguba, near Chinchilla. We also had the privilege of having Mr Jarrett come to teach. After we finished building the school, which was halfway through 1951, we built huts for the returning families.

That whole year was taken up with people returning. The last family and the dormitory girls arrived at the end of the year. We

Hope Vale girls' dormitory

were flat out getting houses ready. The mill was in full production. Timber cutters were camping out at Six Mile. There were two army blitz trucks used to transport timber to the mill. Ted Bowen had ready-cut logs available and when we put in orders for milled timber, it was ready the next day.

The church also brought in painters, builders, mechanics and plumbers. The builder was Wilton Zippel from Lowood and he worked with Trevor Harms and Trevor Dionysus. The plumbers laid pipes and worked out connections. Jack Bambie, Fred Deeral and Tony Flinders worked along with them and learnt the plumbing trade. Two or three men worked along with the mechanic and became skilled, so that they could maintain and repair trucks, tractors and later on cars. The local carpenter trained Chris Woibo. Henry Baru made cement blocks for bathrooms and laundries in the new houses.

Neville Knopke, a cousin of Robert Knopke, arrived from Kingaroy. He was a young builder. He was placed in charge of our team: Jellicoe Jacko, Harry Costello, Uncle Roy Dick, Victor Cobus, Syd and me. Under his supervision, we built the storekeeper's house, the manager's house and a cow shed for Mr Radke, who had milking cows. The storekeeper's house is the last old house still standing in Hope Vale today.

My people want to go home

There wasn't much in the way of sport at Hope Vale. There were football matches on Sunday, and the boys played hockey on the main street. Boxing was begun, but didn't last long. The most popular pastime was hunting for kangaroos, goannas and wild pigs. Of course there were no motor cars, so everyone walked. When I came back from Woorabinda I was very heavy, between fifteen and sixteen stone. I decided to get fit by walking, and sure enough, sweating up and down the mountains did the trick and I lost weight, going down to twelve stone.

I honestly feel that our home was one of the happiest at Hope Vale. Though food was scarce at times, Mum always managed to produce a lovely meal. She never spoke out of place and she always corrected us children when we were naughty. Life was tough in the early years, but she never complained. I do remember one time though when my mother confronted one of the relief pastors. Kathleen had come home with terrible welts on her legs. She could hardly walk! Mum was really wild about this. This pastor was a teacher, and sometimes flogged the little kids.

The pig hunt

This story illustrates the bush skills the older men maintained, despite their years on the mission.

Mitchell McGreen asked me to come with him to kill a pig. It was in the afternoon and I said I thought it was too late. 'No, we'll go,' said Mitchell, 'and we'll take Paul Yoren too.' We took four dogs with us. I had Dad's gun and Mitchell carried his .303. We started walking, turning off at Palm Creek and climbing onto the top of the ridge. By the time we had got down the side of the creek, the sun had gone down. It was pitch black and we couldn't see anything at all. Then the dogs started barking and ran off. 'That's a pig alright,' we said. But it was so dark we were afraid we might shoot one or more of the dogs if we started shooting.

'Leave it to me,' said Mitchell. 'I can see the pig and the dogs.' Bang! The dogs stopped barking and we were sure he'd killed one or more of them. We went forward, feeling our way through the trees. We couldn't see anything until we were almost on top of the pig. It was lying there and the dogs were moving around it. We dragged it out through the shadows, made a fire, gutted it and cut it into portions. Then we heaved it onto our shoulders and started walking. We were home an hour before midnight.

'Ngayu Binaa Ngathu Bubu', I Love My Country, 2007

After many years I was able to make a successful claim on some of my traditional country. To honour my land I painted this picture. I sometimes see brolgas that come to feed in my country. When I go to my land I feel relaxed and happy and I commune with nature. Being there gives me great joy. I feel I have come home, I belong.

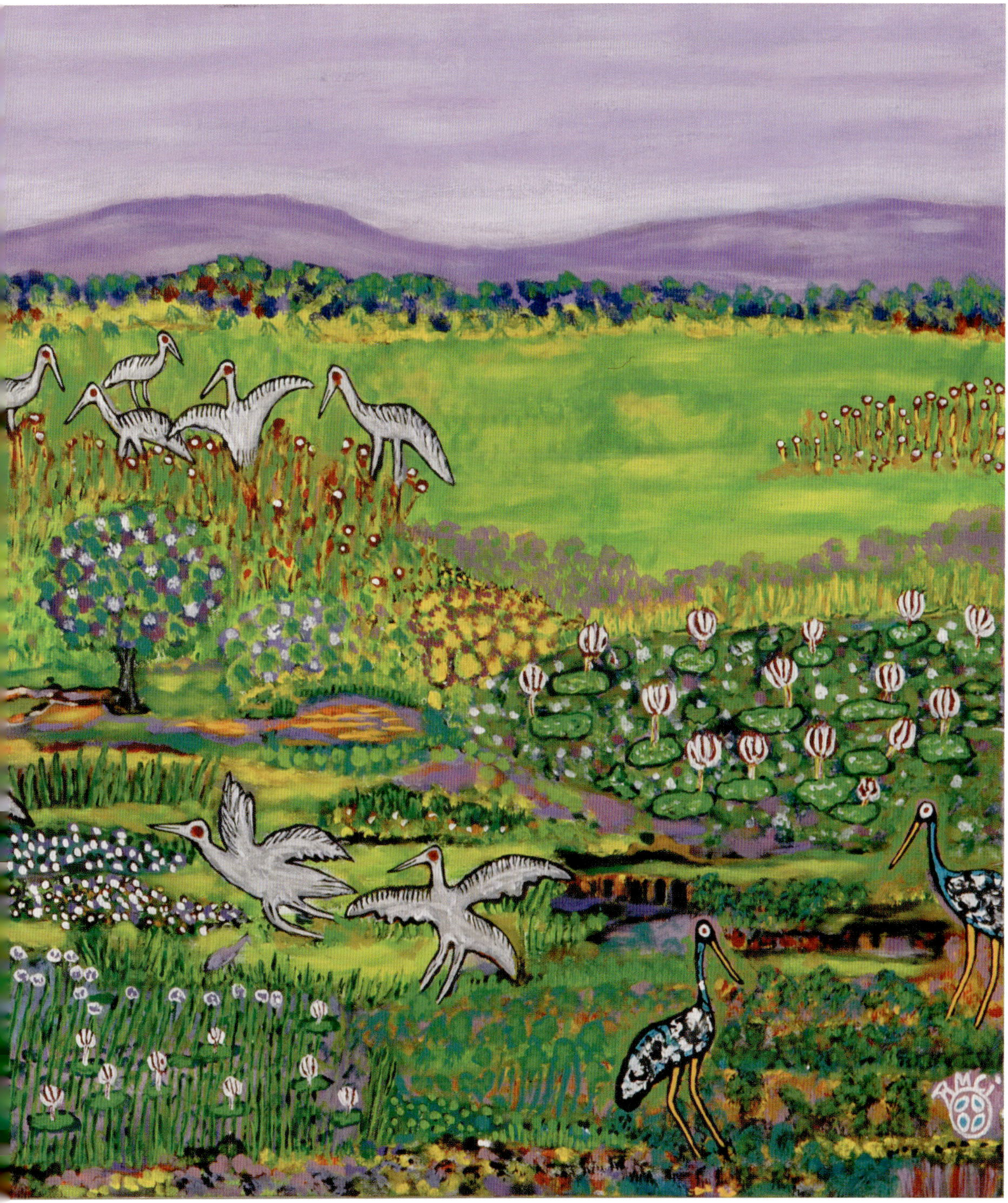

Paddy and Rachel with grandchildren

CHAPTER SEVEN

Establishing Hope Vale

In 1953, at age 85, missionary Muni drove out to Hope Vale in his car to take his last service. There was no minister at the time and my father, Bapa Baru and Ngathi Alick Cameron had been taking the services in Guugu Yimithirr and English. Muni's last words to his congregation that day were, 'I don't regret coming from Germany as a young man and never returning. I have stood by many who were dying and saw they were strong in their faith. My labours were not in vain.' Muni died six years later. He was buried at Hope Vale.

The favourite time of the year was the Christmas holidays when families went down to the beach. After the morning service on Boxing Day, families set off. Everyone, including my mother, the children and the old people walked. With the regular exercise of walking and our naturally healthy diet, everyone was fit.

There was no iron to build huts, so the young people had to strip tea-tree for bark, called buthu. It used to rain a lot, and I

Muni's grave

Muni had followed the command in the Bible: Go ye into all the world and baptise in the name of the Father, Son and Holy Spirit. These were the familiar names from our childhood: God Biba, God Yumuurr, God Wawu Gandaahl, God the Father, God the Son and God the Holy Spirit.

remember sleeping dry and cool in those huts. What started as a fortnight's holiday soon became a month.

Bama still lived under the umbrella of caring and sharing. Families had their huts in distinct areas and the hunters shared their catch. It was a wonderful life and this way of spending our Christmas holidays continued for decades. Today things are different, though families still go down to the beach at holiday time.

One Christmas, I stayed back for a couple of days with Uncle Willie, Jacob Baru and Eric Rosendale. We left Hope Vale at about ten in the morning, carrying our swags and food. We had Uncle Willie's dog, Carlo, with us. Carlo was a champion pig dog and provided food for many bama in the early days.

We crossed Corduroy, the gully with the logs laid down across it, and headed towards Blackwater Creek. There Carlo bailed up a half-sized pig. We killed it, cut up the minha and carried the pieces on our shoulders. We crossed Blackwater and came

Establishing Hope Vale

to Giirnganthin Mountain. Here Carlo chased a pig into the Blackwater scrub. Jacob Baru, whose hearing was poor, couldn't tell which way it had gone. He headed in one direction, Eric in the opposite. Uncle Willie stood his ground and I went for the pig. The pig bailed me up, and I hastily climbed a tree. But the tree had no fork and I kept sliding down, until the pig nearly grabbed my feet. It was a big sow, with no tusks, but it could have bitten me. I was singing out. Finally Jacob came and shot the pig. We cut it up and shared out the load. Now we were humping a big weight.

At Waandarin Gap, Carlo went off towards the creek. This time he bailed up a big spotted boar. Again we killed it, cut it up and lumped the minha onto our aching shoulders.

When we got to the beach, we found that Syd had speared four big stingrays. The women had made buunhjaarr (minced stingray). We pig hunters were hungry! People shared out the buunhjaarr. The pigs we had brought were welcome and everyone had a good feed.

Our family had our first huts at Thalgaar (Deep Creek) and then at Alligator Creek. Dad and Uncle Willie set up huts at Biniirrigu where we shared our time with Aunty Dolly and our cousins, including Monty and Doris, Francis and Ella, Bedford and Mulun Darkan and Uncle Roy Dick with his family. We hunted, fished and gathered food from the land. We went out to Conical Rock in our dinghies, where we hunted turtle and stingray. In later years, we changed from Biniirrigu to a new place, further up the beach.

The church always encouraged us to become self-sufficient and helped bama get land for farming. Our bama certainly knew how to set up vegetable gardens! People grew peanuts and cotton, which were exported down south. The share-farmers working in this enterprise were Charlie McLean, Peter Gibson, Willy Woibo and my father.

Some of the farm work in the fifties was corn-picking and harvesting peanuts. Peanuts were a popular crop in the red soil country of the Endeavour Valley and Hope Vale. The Millers, who lived next door, grew them and employed our workers. Even Mt Webb Station, which was managed by George Rosendale, grew peanuts. The farm we know today as Hazelmere used to be a peanut farm. I worked there by myself and the owner, Mr Kelly, would come out to see how I was going. On some weekends I went into Cooktown with him, where there were picture shows. Other weekends I rode home on my bike. The road wasn't busy. It was only used by the mission truck, the Millers, and a few people who lived near the McIvor and Starcke Rivers — not much traffic! When Billy Jacko stayed with me, it was good to have company.

There were cattle on the mission which were sold to the butcher in Cooktown. Later, the mission did away with the cattle and some of our people took them over. Hope Vale also ran a seed production industry, and when the time came for harvesting, they called on the women. When the Morris brothers took over Hazelmere, some Hope Vale women went out there to help. My godmother, Ann Cameron, kept a meticulous diary, and she records two Bedford trucks taking women out to neighbouring farms to collect seed. Mostly, this was siratro seed, used for cattle fodder. Hazelmere also had a dairy farm on which some of our ladies worked.

The church was also interested in fostering art, and Mr Robert Knopke, from Kingaroy, drew up plans for a shop. Men cut the posts from local timber, set up top rails and an iron roof. This shed was to be the scene of great activity, as tourists travelled by boat from Cairns to Cooktown and Hans Looser drove them out to Hope Vale. They poured into our community art shop, known as the Curio Shop. Everyone was busy making artefacts: dilly bags, mats, hats, boomerangs, nulla nullas, bullroarers, shadow boxes and didgeridoos. The place was buzzing with activity. Syd made and painted many artefacts, and became well-known for his work. Dad, Syd and I built a boat in which we sailed up to the islands and the Starcke River to get turtle and dugong meat. While there, we also collected shells and coral to sell.

Establishing Hope Vale

On 27 August 1956, we started building our church. Neville Knopke was in charge and Gordon Rose, the work manager, chose our team of carpenters: myself, Jellico Jacko, Harry Costello, Syd McIvor, Roy Dick and Victor Cobus. The wood was brought in on blitz trucks. The first stage of the building was the cement foundations. We only had a small cement mixer, but the team worked well. We used a variety of local timbers. Our timber mill could not cut the extra length needed for the tower's timbers, so these were brought in. The timbered section under the windowsills was scrub ironwood, the studs were Moreton Bay ash, the seats were made of pencil pine and the outside wall chamfer boards were puce plum. The floor was black bean and puce plum. The mill always provided timber on demand, and there were no hold-ups. We started on the timber bottom, the top plates, and the tower. We had a good planing machine to plane the timber. This was for the seats, the flooring and the sides up to the bottom of the window frames. On the outside walls we put chamfer boards, made in Hope Vale.

Bark painting

The art was sold through the Curio Shop, and artefacts and bark paintings were sold to 'Aboriginal Creations' in Brisbane, run by the Department of Aboriginal Affairs. My bark paintings are in the Queensland Museum, along with work by Syd, Tulo Gordon, Walter Jack and others.

In 1958 the work was completed, and four very competent painters were called in. They were Uncle Willie, Fred Deeral, and Fred and Jimmy Jacko. The outside walls were finished first and then they proceeded with the inside. They had to varnish the walls up from the floor to the window level and paint the rest to the ceiling. The only wood brought from outside was the wood used for the tower, the altar, the pulpit and the baptismal font. In 1958, there was a big occasion, with lots of visitors, and the Church was opened. At the time, the church building was the biggest Lutheran church in Queensland.

Dad continued to remain a leader in the community. He was multi-skilled and adaptable. Dad had first been taught building, carpentry and boat-building by Mr Nielson whilst living at Cape Bedford, and his skills in these areas were used numerous times over the years with the community's many relocations.

He also maintained his reputation as a great builder. At Woorabinda, he had started carving snake walking sticks, and he continued to make traditional artefacts. He started running a piggery and used to sell his pigs to Norman Palmer, the butcher in Cooktown. He also worked as a guide for the tourists brought out to Hope Vale by Hans Looser. In 1953, Muni offered to sell Dad his car, a utility, but bama on the mission were not allowed to own cars at that time.

We helped Dad clear about five acres of scrub outside town. He planted peanuts, cotton, taro, bananas, pumpkins and pawpaws. When the bottom fell out of the market for peanuts and cotton, he planted more pumpkins and bananas. He used to sell his produce to Bert Olive in Cooktown.

Dad had always been fascinated by new technology, and had friends in Cooktown, Mr and Mrs Miles, who sold kerosene fridges. He was the first bama to buy one of these fridges. He was also the first to buy engines for his boats. Around this time, he bought his first outboard motor, a Swordfish. The dinghies we used were built by my father. He built a lovely clinker rowing boat.

Establishing Hope Vale

Milling the timber

There was no pay for us in the fifties, but sometimes when we had to work on Saturdays we were given six tins of corned beef!

Hope Vale church, 1958

I was delighted to see how beautiful it was. We were only young men when we built this lovely building and it has stood the test of time. I feel a sense of pride as an artist because the church is a work of art.

Church floor

Jellicoe Jacko and I were given the job of laying the church floor. Neville Knopke showed us what to do and left us to it. We laid it down in strips with two planks of puce plum and one of black bean to give a subtle striped effect. Recently, the floor was resurfaced for the 50 years anniversary celebration.

Cockatoo

In front of the Hope Vale church. Left to right: Harry Costello, Paddy McIvor, Pastor Kernich, Baru and Alick Cameron

Dismantling buildings

Dad, Syd, Jellicoe and I were sent out to dismantle buildings in the Cooktown area. One of the buildings was the Great Northern Hotel. This building had survived the 1949 cyclone, though the roof and rafters were gone. We knocked down the rest of the building and stacked the materials. They were quickly taken by someone after we had finished the job. Another job was to remove the fixtures and the furniture inside the prisoner of war camp building. Inside the building, Japanese names had been written on the walls. When we had finished, Sergeant Griffin told us we could keep the basins, tables, chairs and dishes. We were going to take them out on the mission truck after we had finished our next job, which was to build a toilet at Four Mile. However, when we returned a week later, everything was gone. Someone else had taken them in our absence.

We wondered why Cooktown had needed a prisoner of war camp. I was told that while we were in Woorabinda, some Japanese soldiers had been dropped off at the shore near Cape Bedford by a submarine one night. They walked along the beaches and bays and came around to Steamer Beach where they were caught by the local military.

Establishing Hope Vale

My father, Paddy, holding Desmond McIvor (Syd's son), with Hans Looser

Hans used to bring tourists out to Hope Vale and Dad would show them around.

Visiting my father's grave in Cairns

A born entrepreneur, my father was an accomplished, versatile and practical man who could try his hand at anything.

Uncle Willie also built his boats. The one he often used at this time he named 'Wayarego'. Later, Dad bought a couple of British Seagull outboard motors which were very good. We used these to go out to the reef. When other bama saw this, they asked Dad to order motors for them. No one had much money, but they managed to save up to buy these motors. Uncle Willie bought one too. Dad loved working with boats. He had enjoyed his time working as a captain and a seaman. He had a lovely sailing boat called the 'Louanna'. We took the Louanna north from Cape Flattery into crocodile country. Dad, David Deemal, Syd and I were there shooting crocodiles. We went crocodile hunting a few times as we sold the skins to a shop in Port Douglas.

When I think of my father, I picture him in the little workshop he had set apart from the house, where he used to make all sorts of things. He collected bark from messmate trees so I could make bark paintings. He cut blocks of Cooktown ironwood to carve birds and animals. Mum used to call him into the house for smoko, and growl at him when he was too absorbed in his work to come for his meals.

My father died in Cairns Base Hospital on 24 December 1967. Mum had passed away earlier in that year. Dad was buried in Cairns. For all his service to his community, it was very sad that we could not afford to bury Dad at Hope Vale.

The Restless Years

During the sixties, we had to leave Hope Vale and go out and look for work. I travelled around Queensland working at many different jobs, which often meant hard work and long hours for very little pay.

My first trip was to Palm Island with Hans Pearson. Palm Island was a cohesive, peaceful community, with lovely gardens. The police were local people and the place was controlled in a good way and there was no alcohol abuse. We got work cleaning around banana plants until word got out that I was a carpenter and I got work with a man from Wujal Wujal. We stayed in the community where I went to the Baptist church. There were familiar faces and we surprised the locals by calling out to each other in Guugu Yimithirr.

Later I went to Rokeby Station, west of Coen, with Arthur McGreen and Charlie Pearson to build a work shed with a shop area inside. There was no chainsaw, though we had a Blitz truck to collect the logs. Even though the shed was completely made with bush materials, it was a perfectly finished building. When I went back to Coen years later I took Thelma and the kids to see the shed I'd built. It was a sound building and it made me happy to see it again. Arthur and I were there for eight months and we got on well with the other men. Some of them were real bushmen. I was not, and always needed their guidance.

There was an arrowroot farm owned by Lutheran people at Upper Coomera, Mr Kleinschmidt and his sons. The church sent eight of us down there to work. Henry Baru and I started in the factory. It was hard work and we kept at it for three or four months. When I got home, I discovered there was only twenty-two dollars for me at the office for all those months of hard labour. We went back the following year and, again, it was hard work for little money. Next we got a building job in Brisbane – we worked from sunrise to sunset and were paid twelve dollars a week.

In Brisbane we saw lines of men queuing up at the employment office. We decided to go down the street and ask if anyone had any work and finally we were signed on with the Theiss Company. We went to Fortitude Valley in Brisbane by train the next day. The boss picked us up and took us to a job at Pinkenba, where the ships come into the river. We were building foundations there. We had a good boss and were paid weekly at award wages. This was the first decent pay in our lives and after Pinkenba we went to Cooper's Plains to lay pipes, which were so big you can stand up in them without having to bend your head — I also went to Salisbury to lay pipes and worked at the cement works at Darra, where our last job was to build an elevator to carry coral from the boat to the cement works. We worked until Christmas. We got our holiday pay and went home. Uncle Roy Dick and I got

Cockatoo

Working on the arrowroot farm

There was an arrowroot farm owned by Lutheran people at Upper Coomera, a Mr Kleinschmidt and his sons. The church sent eight of us down there to work.

a job with the Smart Brothers from Cairns. We built the twelve houses for them and received good pay for our work.

I went to stay with my sister Dorothy and Len at Bundaberg. The first job I found was on a farm, picking strawberries and beans. The next was a job with a cabinet-making place. I had to clean up, pick up shavings and waste timber, and load this onto the truck. I had to do that before I got into the real work of cabinet making. They asked me to get a driver's licence to take the truck to the dump. After that I could start to do the cabinet making. But I didn't get the licence, and I lost the job — we were still 'living under the Act' and permission to own cars was not given until 1971. I got my licence in about 1974, Syd taught me to drive along the Hope Vale roads.

In 1966 a silica sand mine started up at Cape Flattery and almost the whole Hope Vale workforce ended up there. I went up when they were pegging out the first area to be mined. There were a lot of men and we all camped in tents. My cousin Monty and I often went spearing mullet and other fish, which we cooked up on the beach.

Roger Yoren and I were chosen to be crew members of the launch that delivered the bags of sand from Cape Flattery to the wharf at Cooktown. A bag of sand, the size of a cement bag, was very heavy! At the mining site they were loaded onto a truck, which took them to the beach, where they were loaded onto a dinghy.

The dinghy took the bags of sand out to the boat. The process of loading and unloading was heavy work. Mr Beggs, who did not sail himself, took no heed of the weather. When it was bad we still had to set off in headwinds of up to 30 knots. The boat was loaded in the afternoon and didn't finish until 5 or 6. We left when the boat was full and did not arrive into Cooktown until late that night. Walter Jack and Toby Jacko helped us unload the sandbags onto the wharf in the morning. When the tide was high, this work was much easier — at low tide, it was back-breaking work. We received very little money for this hard labour. At Cape Flattery there were decent houses for the manager and the foremen but our living and cooking quarters were no good as the rain came in.

A jetty and conveyor belt were built and ships from Japan started to arrive. With the new conveyor belt, there was no need for many labourers, so we were told to go home. After we left, Cape Flattery started making money and could hire permanent workers. They started to build houses for their workers.

When I heard that jobs were being offered at Fairymead, near Bundaberg, I rode my bike out there and they took me on. The job was feeding clean, cut cane into a machine which cut it into pieces for planting. The work wasn't hard and it paid well.

After that, I went south and worked on the Hack's sugar mill and then did odd jobs on farms on the Cape. I was thinking I would like a spell from travelling and concentrate on painting, mainly bark painting and making wooden artefacts. Near the start of 1972, my friend Henry and I decided to finish with working outside and to settle in Hope Vale.

'Maji bithaaygu buliili' #1, Raindrops 1, 2007

When you look at nature in the tropics, there are two seasons: wet and dry. In the dry it appears that things are dying. Plants die and the earth gets parched and cracks up. But when the rain comes, the Wet, almost immediately the earth springs back to life. The power of the raindrop is renewal. All nature sings again. A sparkle comes back to life forms, everything becomes beautiful, flowers bloom expressing glorious new colour and life. Nature survives once again.

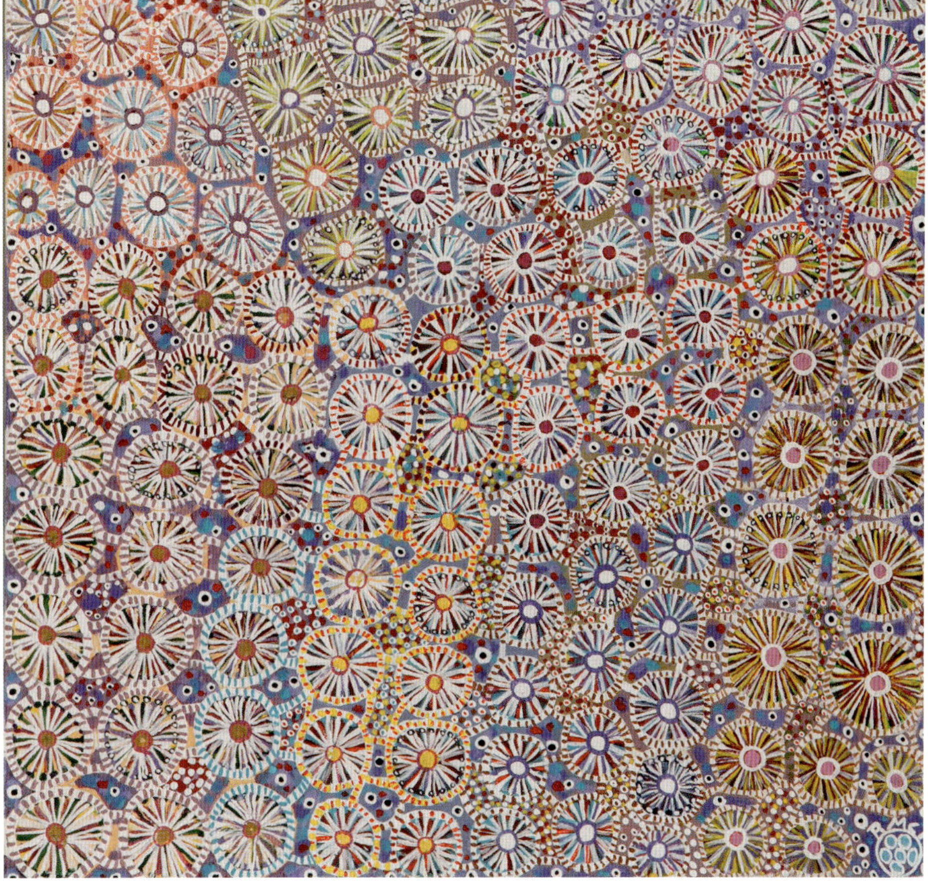

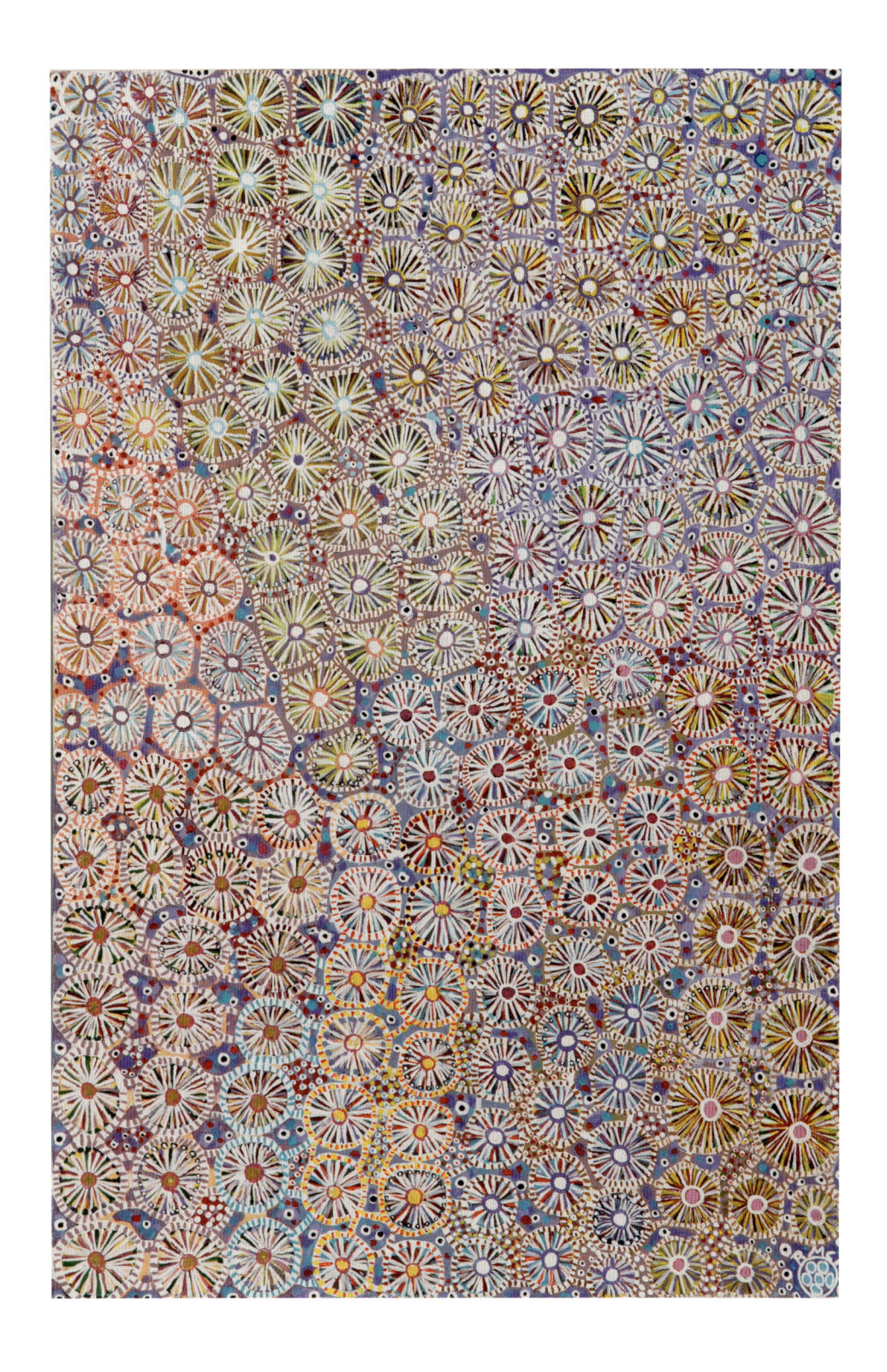

Our wedding

When Thelma and I were married, there had been a few mixed-race marriages in those days, but we were the first mixed-race couple that was allowed to stay living in Hope Vale after our marriage.

CHAPTER EIGHT

Sing a song of love

The urge to meet someone I could settle down with grew stronger. I had met a few nice ladies in the past, but I had never been seriously romantically involved. I first saw Thelma in January of 1972 while she was walking to the artefact shop. Thelma had travelled to Hope Vale to work as a teacher. Her family was Lutheran and she had grown up in South Australia. She had travelled a long way to get here! I thought she was beautiful, but I didn't know how to approach her. My friend Henry Baru helped me out — there was mail for her. He told me to give it to her and he also said that I would find her in the school doing schoolwork at night time. I plucked up the courage that night to give her the mail, and nervously handed it over to her. She thanked me kindly and offered me a chair. We sat and talked and I secretly could not help admiring her youth and beauty. When it was time to go, I told her I would like to see her again. 'You're welcome' she said warmly.

The next time I saw Thelma, I brought my guitar and played her love songs from the fifties. She loved it and I offered to teach her to play the guitar. She eagerly accepted and I started seeing more

Posing with my guitar

I got to see more of Thelma by offering to teach her to play the guitar. I played her love songs from the fifties.

of her. Soon we admitted our mutual attraction, and we shared our first kiss. We went on adventures together, though always in the company of good friends. Lester Rosendale had a Volkswagen and one day he took us fishing at Hans Pearson's place at Poison Creek. While we were there, it started raining, so we headed back home. Bustard Park was flooded on our way back, so we had to wait a couple of hours for the water to go down. Another time we went for a picnic and fishing at Leggett's. When we wanted to get married, I sent a letter to Thelma's parents in which I asked for their daughter's hand. Though they were a bit reluctant at first, they gave us their consent. By this time, my parents had died and so they never met Thelma.

We were married on 9 December 1972. Henry Baru and Chris Woibo were the best men and the bridesmaids were June Pearson, Ora Pohlner and Thelma's sister, Lyn. There had been a few mixed-race marriages in those days, but we were the first mixed-race couple that was allowed to stay living in Hope Vale after our marriage. We had to apply for permission, and Eric Deeral, as Chairman of the Council, helped us. Thelma had trained as a teacher in Adelaide and had done practice teaching at the Lutheran mission at Hermannsburg near Alice Springs. Hope Vale was short of teachers and Thelma had been requested

Sing a song of love

Thelma teaching singing

Thelma had travelled from South Australia to be at Hope Vale — I thought she was beautiful.

to come. She had come alone to Far North Queensland, being delayed by a cyclone in Townsville, and had been driven out to Hope Vale by truck. Thelma got ill soon after arriving, and was unable to teach full-time for about six weeks. After we were married, Thelma continued to work as a relief teacher for a while.

Our daughter Ramona was born in 1974. She was named after the mission boat and also after an old song which came to Thelma's mind. Thelma had to travel to Cairns four weeks before the due date, which all expectant mothers had to do for their first birth, as there were no emergency maternity facilities in our area. Two years later, our son, Selwyn, was born in Cooktown.

All this while, I had been making and selling artefacts. The church was actively encouraging private enterprise in the community and I decided to make a go of my art. I got a loan from the Aboriginal Development Commission to buy a band saw, a circular saw and a sander. I built a building from bush materials. Harold Ford helped me with the cementing, and when it was finished, I opened my own shop! I made boomerangs, shields, nulla nullas and lots of other artefacts. Thelma and I went out collecting bush materials, scouring the hillsides for hollow saplings for didgeridoos. Business was going so well that I could not keep up with the customers' demands. Busloads of tourists started coming up from Mossman. I was toying with the idea of buying artefacts from others to sell, but then the rules changed and tourists had to apply for a permit to visit our community. The flow of tourists decreased dramatically. A sign to apply for permission to visit the mission deterred the tourists even more.

Thelma

In the days of the art shop, Thelma was moved to see how warmly and graciously Roy welcomed the tourists. She was aware that white people were searching for meaningful contact with Aboriginal people and their traditions. She saw Roy, and his father before him, as true cultural ambassadors.

Artefacts made at home in the late 1980s

I continued to sell my art through the Curio Shop, and took up working there with Syd. We also did cabinet making jobs, making cupboards, sink cabinets and coffins. Coffins were made from silky pine. There were six of us working and we were busy all the time.

Sing a song of love

My private art shop with the variety of artefacts I made and sold during the 1980s

With Thelma in the curio shop

Thelma saw Roy, and his father before him, as true cultural ambassadors.

Cockatoo

Our business suffered a blow, so much that we had to close the shop. I continued to sell my art through the Curio Shop, and took up working there with Syd. We also did cabinet making jobs, making cupboards, sink cabinets and coffins. Coffins were made from milky pine. There were six of us working and we were busy all the time.

One Christmas holiday, we went to Mt Saunders with Dorothy's family. We went by boat to the North Shore. Thelma and the kids set up camp while I took the boat back across the river to pick up Dorothy and her husband Len. After we returned and everyone had set up camp, we went fishing. It was a horrible night, as the place was alive with mosquitoes. The following day we packed up and headed home.

We were certainly in for an adventure on a different holiday! We were camping with Dorothy and Len at the Annan River. This was a good spot without too many mosquitoes. We had been there for some time when Len and Dorothy left to get supplies and to spend the weekend at their home. My other sister Kathy, her husband Johnny and their children decided to join us. By late afternoon,

Mt Saunders

We had a memorable Christmas holiday at Mt Saunders with Dorothy's family.

the wind had picked up and it had started raining. It was not long before we were drenched and the wind picked up even more. The wind was now so strong it bent the sheoaks' branches until they almost touched the ground! Johnny and Kathy's tent collapsed with them and their kids in it, so they had to shelter with us.

We were camped in a small timber and corrugated iron lean-to, which somebody had built. We put a tarp around it and were quite cosy and dry. There wasn't enough space for us to lie down, so we sat huddled together. The wind howled and the rain poured down. The next morning, the river had swollen. We'd had sixteen inches of rain and the river was huge and raging. The water was eight feet over the old Annan Bridge, and we were worried about our cars parked on the other side.

Johnny was stressed and very restless, and he insisted on leaving. We all got in the boat, two families with young children in a twelve-foot plywood dinghy in raging flood waters. It was horrendous! I managed to dodge the tree trunks as I took the boat upstream, but I wasn't able to get the boat across to the other side, as the current was too strong. I took the boat back downstream, where I was able to get across near the mouth of the Annan.

Here we met Jerry Brandt, Ronnie Palmer and some of their friends, who had come out to look at the flood waters. They told us about an approaching cyclone. I said, 'I don't think that cyclone is going to hit us. We had it last night!' We had survived the night through a cyclone in a small hut. Even though we had been camping close to Cooktown, the wind there had not been unusually strong.

The men gave us a lift into town. They offered to swim across the floodwaters near Keating's Lagoon with ropes to check on our cars, but I declined their offer. A car can be replaced but not a life. The next day the floodwaters had receded and we managed to get to our cars. We were amazed to find they were still there, parked on the low bank above the Annan River. It seemed a miracle that they had stayed on dry land, parked so close to the river through the floods.

In 1967, award wages were granted and by 1971, alcohol was legally available to Aboriginal people. Because they had to be

Thelma and I in front of the old house

paid award wages, many Aboriginal stockmen who were formerly employed on cattle stations in Cape York, found themselves unemployed and homeless. Some with family ties came to live at Hope Vale. Alcohol did not seem to be an immediate problem, but its effects were ominous.

By the early seventies, many things had changed. The last vestiges of the Act were removed. The power of the church finished up and we got a community council. Self-management through an elected council sounded good, but at times it led to nepotism, rivalry and ill-feeling between families.

At Woorabinda we had worked for wages, even though these had been very low. When we came back to Hope Vale it was rations again and the church encouraged people to make their own money. When welfare payments were introduced, these small regular payments provided us with a bit of extra pocket-money.

Some members of the church tried to apply rules to make us adhere to the old ways of sharing. It got to the point where individuals were ruling how hunters from Hope Vale had to share their kill! Henry Baru had a wild reaction to this when he was confronted by one staff member who accused him of not sharing. He had shared his kill with his family, but the way the staff member viewed sharing obviously clashed with ours.

Thelma and I were living in the old house built by my father, Syd and me. We wanted the security of knowing that we could stay there. Des Pietsch was a member of the Lutheran Mission Board and an officer in the Department of Aboriginal Affairs who worked at Hope Vale. He acted as a liaison between the church and the government. Des suggested that we secure a lease on the land. Little did we realise that this would require a special Act of Parliament! The deed was signed in October 1977, the first such lease on Aboriginal Reserve land in Queensland.

Changing times

Some of the social changes were discussed by bama in their local paper, the 'Hope Vale Hotline'. In August 1974, Lester Rosendale wrote a letter to the editor, entitled 'What is Hope Vale?' in which he says, 'Hope Vale is fast becoming like other communities, for we have gambling, drunken brawls and everything that goes with it.'

A year later, George Rosendale gave a report to a Convention of the Lutheran Church in Bundaberg, which voiced the frustration of bama feeling increasingly disempowered. 'At Hope Vale the people want to do things. They want to build their own houses instead of sitting down while the government does. And they want the opportunity to buy these houses.'

'Buurraay thabulthabul', Sacred waterhole, 2006

I was going back to my country and on the way stopped by the sacred waterhole. This waterhole is said to be the site where the Creator Spirit, the Rainbow Serpent, returned to rest after moving over the land creating all that is.

Indigenous people had serious respect for such sacred places and considered it taboo for many regular activities such as swimming. Anyone who participated in such activities got sick.

I sat near the waterhole and meditated, needing some inspiration for painting. Quite soon a picture started emerging in my mind. I did a brief sketch and took some notes. When I got home I started painting. This painting is as I saw it. There was no struggle in painting this picture.

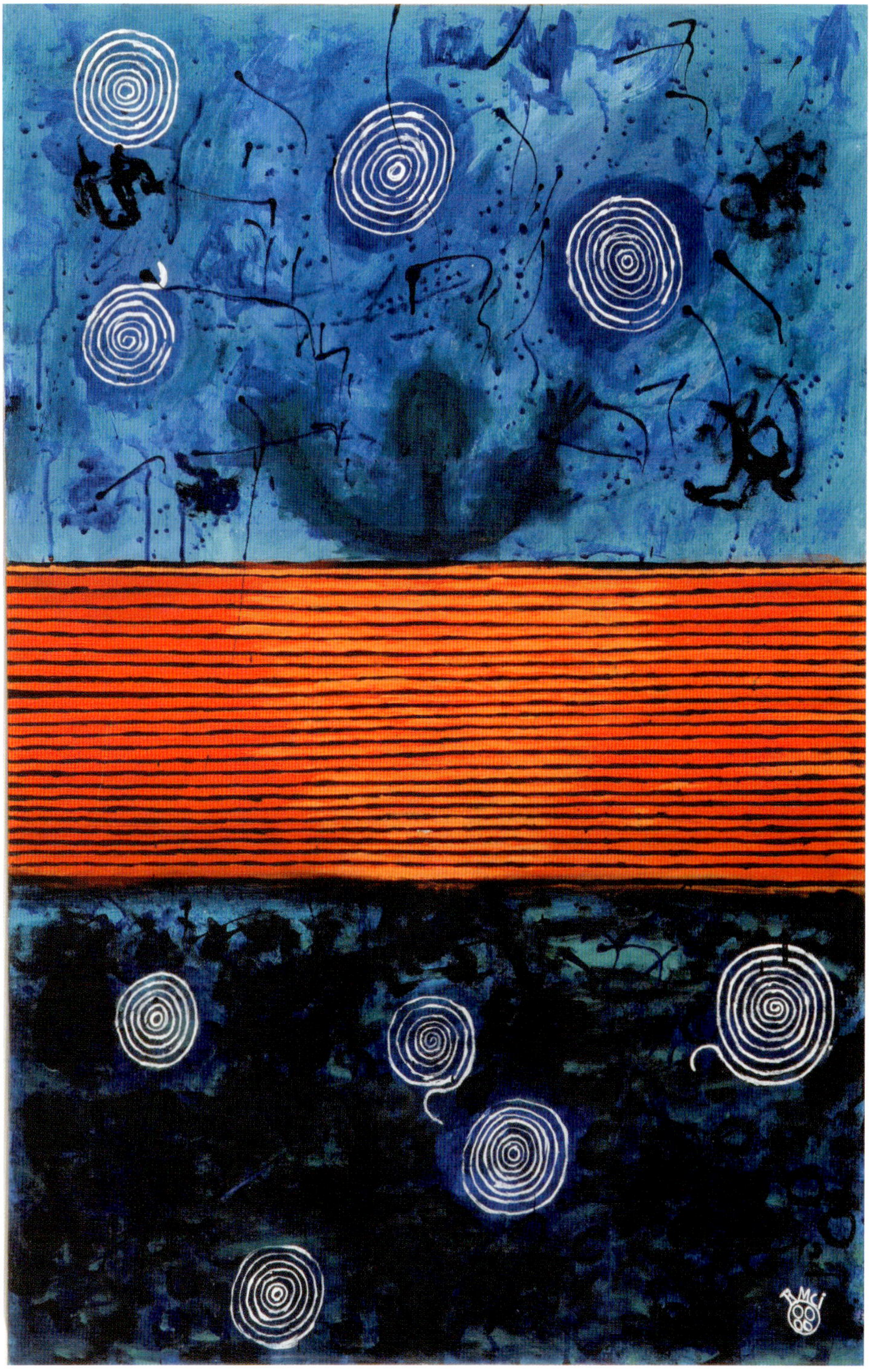

'Dawaar',
Morning star, 2004

In Guugu Yimithirr, the name of the morning star is Dawaar. It is seen in the eastern sky as people are starting to move, ready to walk from the camp or go hunting. Just before dawn is also the time when thuga, the scrub-hen, sings the last of its night calls. Dawaar is a symbol I use in many of my paintings.

CHAPTER NINE

Call to church

I had been confirmed in 1960, and had become involved in church work. At first I was a Sunday school teacher and a steward of the church. Being a steward involved helping with the preparation of services, ringing the bell, lighting the candles and managing the collection. I also worked at church busy bees, and sang as a tenor in the choir. We had a wonderful choir, which sung in the four parts of bass, tenor, alto and soprano.

When I was Chairman of the Church Council, I enjoyed the travel and meeting people. The experience I gained gave me confidence and I learnt to speak well in public. Before that, I couldn't say boo!

Teaching Sunday school was another matter. When I first started, I met with the pastor to discuss the classes. I took my first lessons but the children were difficult, and I felt that I couldn't express myself well. I went to Elmore Kotzur and explained my difficulties. He simply asked me, 'Have you called on the Holy Spirit for strength, courage and understanding?' So I went away and I did ask for guidance. I found I was more confident with the children and became a successful teacher. My mind also went back to Muni and I drew inspiration from his example.

Cockatoo

Pastor Sheldahl and myself

I was also Chairman of the Church Council, and a representative for Hope Vale at Church Synods in Brisbane and elsewhere. I reported on the work of the church in Hope Vale and in outlying areas like Wujal Wujal and Coen.

Dreams

In more recent times, I had a vision. In my dream, it was around midnight. It was very quiet. A bright light appeared on the horizon. I heard Victor Cobus crying out, 'There is a light coming!' The light was headed for our old school building and hit the black board in the schoolroom. I was right at the front door. In the middle of the light, the shadow of Jesus appeared. All I could see was his head wearing the crown of thorns he was given on the day he was crucified. His image grew clearer as he stepped out of the old school. He was wearing white and his face shone brightly. Where Jesus was standing, the night sky was a light blue as in daytime. I could see the Alexandra Palms clearly as they became visible in the bright light. The palms and the most beautiful flowers quickly grew up around us. People came from everywhere to gather around Jesus who was pleased to see everyone and he talked to all. He nursed the children who were very happy to see him. Some people shied away from him crying, 'I am not ready yet'. When he finished talking, he started floating upwards. The light faded as he got further away from us. 'Be ready for when I come back. I will return as judge. Prepare yourselves!' I last heard him say. As he disappeared, the light faded and we were back in the night's darkness. It was a most beautiful scene which I will never forget.

In the late sixties, Pastor Albrecht came to Hope Vale. He encouraged Indigenous churchmen to become evangelists, and eventually, pastors. George Rosendale, Alick Cameron and Harry Costello had been ordained.

Pastor Sheldahl came in 1982. He was a great inspiration, and was keen to train more bama for the ministry. Mulun Darkan and I were considering this training. Pastor Sheldahl gave us encouragement, and he took a community survey, which gave us good support. But becoming a pastor involved leaving the family while I studied in South Australia and New Guinea. I would then possibly have to serve in New Guinea. I thought this might be impractical for my family. Instead, I later went as an evangelist to Coen.

Pastor George Rosendale and his wife Maudie had gone to Coen in 1966, as the first evangelists. They were ready for a change, and in 1982 the church asked if I wanted to take Pastor George's place. Coen was a small town north-west with a population of about 200 people. Approximately 150 of them were Aboriginal. Men from Coen used to go out to work on the cattle stations, which was still strong in the 1980s.

I travelled to Coen with Pastor Paul Loehe, Fred Deeral, Mulun Darkan and Uncle Roy Dick. Barry Port, his wife and their children were living in the church house and they welcomed us in. We stayed there for the weekend and I fell in love with the place. On returning home, I asked Thelma, 'How about a change? I think it will do us good.' She agreed, so we moved with our small children, Ramona and Selwyn.

Bush medicine
There was always a lot of heavy work to do. About three months before we left for Coen, I began to experience an excruciating pain in my back. I saw a specialist, who thought I would have to have an operation. I tried every remedy, to no effect. Then Jack Harrigan, a local bush medicine man, gave me an old recipe. I had to take some bark from a particular tree and boil it up, fill a tub with water, including the boiled bark, and soak in this mixture. I did this every day for a fortnight. The treatment was successful and the pain disappeared. I have never had further problems with my back.

Cockatoo

The Rosendale family

The church gave us a farewell service, where I was commissioned as an evangelist, and presented with a very heavy volume of Kranhz on Church teachings. It was difficult for me to read and not very relevant to my work at Coen!

We tried to pack as much as we could in our small Daihatsu four-wheel-drive, but the Daihatsu was too small for all our gear, so we got a box trailer and loaded it to the brim. Pastor George Rosendale travelled with us in his dual cab. The road was rough and dusty, but everything went well until we got to Kings Plains on the way to Lakeland. As I was driving, I noticed a wheel overtaking us. I was a little puzzled about where that wheel came from, but then the trailer started to swing. We all stopped and saw the trailer's wheel had broken off. We unloaded the trailer, and placed it on its side off the road. Somehow, we managed to cram all the gear into Pastor George's truck and our little car.

In Coen, everyone called us Uncle and Auntie, or Granddad and Grandma. We had family connections through my grandmother. She came from the coast north of the McIvor River and her father had links with the Lamalama people. There was a mixture of tribal groups in the Coen area: Wik Mungkan, Lamalama, Ayapathu, Olkala, Umpila and Kaanju. The kinship relationships were strongly valued.

Packed for Coen, left to right, George Rosendale, Ramona, Selwyn, Thelma and myself

Although people were poor and lived hard lives, there was only periodic drunkenness and little crime. I used to go to different homes for devotions. I was always well-received and treated with respect. I took all the church and burial services, with the exception of marriages. Services were held on the front verandah of our house. This little chapel area was full every Sunday, and a lot of kids came to the Sunday school. Father Tony Hall-Matthews, the flying padre, would visit now and then. He was a great pilot. He was with the Anglican Church and we would attend his services, held at the Australian Inland Mission hostel. Father Hall-Matthews later became Bishop.

Life was expensive at Coen, and our income was low. We added to our small income by selling my artefacts and bark paintings. Thelma got a job at the kindergarten, which helped to pay the bills. Under her direction, the kindergarten progressed from being run by Aboriginal Affairs to being properly accredited. This meant that it could now be staffed by trained teachers.

Pastor Prenzler, who had come to Hope Vale after the Sheldahls left, was interested in the need to deal with social issues in his ministry. He had set up the rehabilitation centre on the McIvor. With his help, we asked the Lutheran Church if we could build a chapel at Coen. The Hope Vale Church Council, Synod and the Lutheran Layman's League discussed the proposal. It was agreed that a new chapel was necessary for the continuation of the

Cockatoo

church's work in Coen. This work would be done by Aboriginal pastors from Hope Vale in the future.

The chapel was a simple structure. There was a cement floor and the walls were painted metal sheets on a steel frame. There were two sliding doors at the front and the back. The materials were carted up to Coen from Cairns on David Deemal's truck. We unloaded them with a forklift. Keith Scholtz, a previous manager from Hope Vale, was the builder in charge. I built the altar from matchwood, a local timber. I also made a big boomerang from a wattle wood. The boomerang hung on the wall above the altar. Laurie Mirtschin from Toowoomba did the electrical work. Mr Frankie was an engineer who supervised the steel work. His wife Joyce did the cooking, with help from Thelma. Several young men from Coen helped with the concreting and the building. Another worker was Paulie Hart from Hope Vale.

During the building, we used to provide a big feed for the workers. This was set out on tables outside. Joyce and Thelma also used a gurrma (underground oven) to cook chicken and vegetables. At Christmas, we had a party at the church house and cooked turtle, kangaroo and pig in this oven.

One of the Elders, Rosie Ahlers suggested that we call the chapel, Thuunbi, the Morning Star. Dr Steike, the President-General of the Lutheran Church of Australia, carried out the official opening, and people came from Hope Vale, Aurukun and Lockhart River.

Thuunbi Dawaar

An elderly traditional woman, Rosie Ahlers, told us the story of the morning star, called Thuunbi in her language. This was an ancient story of conflict between the forces of good and evil. A fearless warrior won a great victory over evil. He died, and was taken up into the sky, where he was transformed into the morning star. This tale had strong parallels with the Christian story of redemption through the death of Jesus and the star over Bethlehem. We decided to call the chapel by the name of the morning star.

Some people would walk to our services, but others I needed to pick up by car. The children called me Grandpa Roy or Uncle Roy, and I remember one day after Sunday school, a couple of boys pointed up to the sky, 'Uncle Roy, blue sky there. We want rain. We haven't had rain for a long time. We want you to pray for rain.' So I prayed for rain, because we were in need of it, then we all went home. About an hour later, it started pouring. Later that evening, those two boys came to see me. 'Uncle Roy, God heard your prayer. It really rained, big rain came!' Other kids said the same the next Sunday. They were impressed with the good rain we had after that prayer!

We had pool tables at the chapel and the youngsters would come to play. Ballgames were organised as well. Sometimes we got the guurrma going. There was a lot of interest in these get-togethers, especially when we had a sing-along, and I played the guitar.

I taught Selwyn to hunt, and we used to go out for kangaroo and pig. On weekends we took people fishing at the Archer River or over to Port Stewart, in Lama Lama country. We had a little dog, called Twinkle, a cross between a dachshund and a poodle. One time when we were pigging, a boar was going to attack Selwyn. It was a dangerous situation as Selwyn was holding the pig off with the butt of his rifle. Twinkle shot up to the boar, barking and growling. The boar got a fright and took off. It was a funny sight to see that harmless little dog bailing up and terrifying such a big boar! We shared our catch with the old people on the reserve. They were always happy to have a pig or kangaroo delivered.

Soon after we arrived, the people asked for my help in setting up an organisation to lobby the government for improved services. We called it Mulpa Kincha and I became its chairman. We started having meetings, but nobody really knew what to talk about. They had never expressed their need to be recognised as people with rights and a history. It took time for them to develop the confidence to do this. I explained that there were land issues to talk about. Through the organisation we could apply for funding from the Department for Aboriginal Affairs, though as yet nobody had come up to discuss our issues. Professor Bruce Rigsby, from the University of Queensland in Brisbane, started coming up and talked about the land with us.

After a few years, the Mulpa Kincha organisation was recognised by the Department of Aboriginal Affairs in Cairns. Two officers came up from Cairns, but people were unsure how to approach them, so I talked. As time went on, people came out of their shell and started talking bit by bit, slowly, slowly until they became real speakers and spoke up about their issues.

By 1987, there were differences of opinion between the members of Mulpa Kincha. The Moomba Aboriginal Corporation was formed, and we continued with our work. The aims of the two organisations were similar, but there were divisions between families. Alcohol problems were increasing and we encouraged people to have a dream of returning to their relatives' lands. Then amazing things began to happen. One by one the four clan groups — Wik Mungkan, Lama Lama, Kaanju and Olkala — got some of their lands back. People had the option to settle on their traditional land and work cattle on their blocks.

Woompi Kepple was leader of the Wik Mungkan people. They wanted Meripah Station and they asked Thelma and me to write to the government. We had regular meetings talking about Meripah, and we saw results. The government bought Meripah Station to hand back to the Wik Mungkan people, and the Minister for Aboriginal Affairs came up for a handing-over celebration. The Department of Aboriginal Affairs made arrangements for families to camp at Meripah where there were good buildings to use. Some workers stayed in Coen for weekends and I drove them back to Meripah on Monday morning. It was a three to four hour drive. This could be dangerous as there were often brumbies on the road. Once I nearly ran into a big black stallion. I had no time to take it easy. I was busy with church work and helping people.

Professor Rigsby, Thelma and I also met with the Lama Lama people to help them with claims in the Port Stewart area. Sunlight Bassani was their Chairman. I went out there and built

Call to church

The policing kangaroo

During our time in Coen, we looked after a young male grey kangaroo which we named Rocky. As Rocky was growing bigger, he started helping himself to the Weetbix in the kitchen. He could reach the higher shelves and look through the boxes to help himself. He was getting cheekier with me too. He kicked me in the chest one day, and I was worried about his sharp claws, though he did not use them. He was only playing around. On the opening day of the chapel, we had a party and some girls were getting heated up and ready to fight. Rocky jumped in and went straight for the troublemaker and knocked her clean over. Everybody had a good laugh at the policing kangaroo!

One day Rocky bounded around the house through the garden until at last, he jumped on the swing, which was made of a car tyre. He swung forwards and backwards, and on the next forward swing, he jumped off and leaped into the bush. This must have been his way of saying goodbye, as we never saw him again. He was still wearing the brown dog collar we had put around his neck.

Selwyn and I pig hunting

I taught Selwyn to hunt, and we used to go out for kangaroo and pig. We shared our catch with the old people living on the reserve. They were always very happy to have a pig or kangaroo delivered.

tank stands and toilets. Their claims were eventually successful and land, including Silver Plains Station, was handed over. There were others we helped, and when the Kaanju people wanted the land near the Wenlock River, we began negotiating. We had started building some bush structures there, but we left Coen before they were completed.

We also helped write letters for the Olkala people in their claim for Glen Garland Station. Cecil Sellars was their leading Elder. After we left Coen, they were also successful. Ross Rolfe, a top bureaucrat, helped us in our negotiations, notably through Anna Bligh who was then a Member of Parliament. These land settlements were amazing achievements because politically all forms of Indigenous land rights were unheard of at the time. However, it happened at Coen.

Thelma worked in the office, set up in the chapel adjoining the church. There was a phone there and she helped people get their money from social security. We also set up a Home and Community Care program (HACC) with the aid of a visiting manager and Coen's local nursing sisters. We then employed Margaret Sellers through HACC to look after the elderly and sick at home.

Elroy's baptism

Elroy was born in 1988 and once again, Thelma had to travel down to Cairns to give birth.

When Ramona and Selwyn were ready for secondary school, they went to St Peter's Lutheran College in Brisbane. At times, in the school holidays, we went to Cairns, visiting Hope Vale on the way back to Coen. Thelma became pregnant once more. Our youngest son Elroy was born in 1988 and once again, Thelma had to travel down to Cairns to give birth.

In 1990, I was diagnosed with a heart problem. I flew to Brisbane from Coen for a couple of weeks and had a triple by-pass operation. I was very grateful it was successful, and thankful to see Thelma and the children by my bedside when I woke up. We flew back to Coen, four days after the operation. But the place where they had cut a vein from my leg for the operation became infected. The sister from the local hospital gave me antibiotic tablets, and my leg healed. I was soon mowing the lawn and cutting logs for the tank stand at the chapel and working at Port Stewart. My illness helped us to decide it was time to return to Hope Vale.

Mt Baird, early morning

Mt Baird Station had been neglected for years and was overrun by the weed, sickle pod. A few years after the acquisition of the station, I saw seven brolgas merrily walking on Mt Baird. It was such a happy sight. Brolgas are dancing birds respected by all Guugu Yimithirr. I have never heard of one of these birds being killed by any Guugu Yimithirr. When I saw the birds, I knew Mt Baird was back in balance.

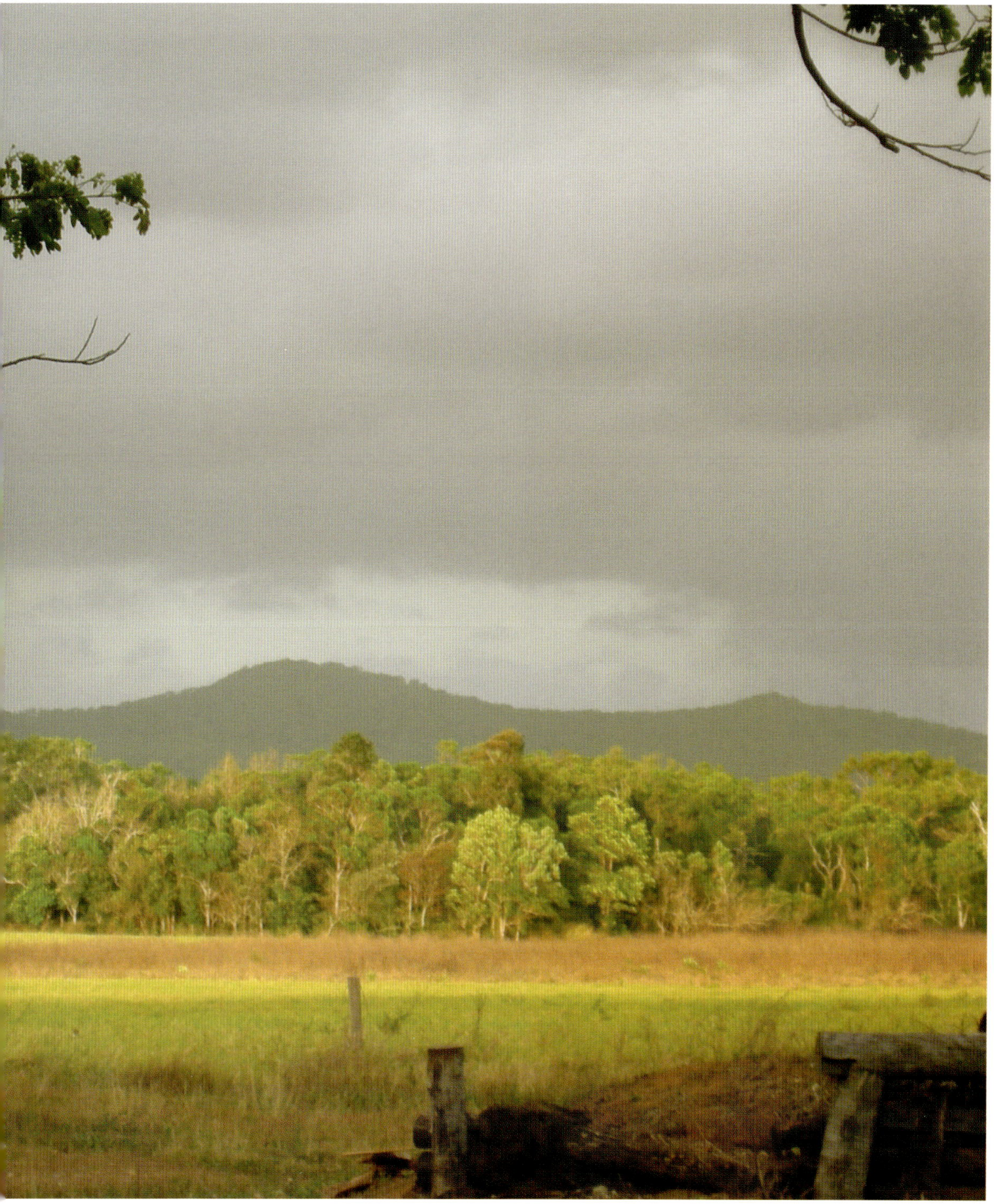

'Binthi minhangay gajarrmu',
Binthi increase ceremony, 2004

Aboriginal people have always belonged to the land.

CHAPTER TEN

Return to Hope Vale

Our time in Coen had been very enjoyable. We had lived in a roomy house, and were sad to leave. With our car packed, we returned to Hope Vale. I had to make two trips as we could not fit everyone and everything into the car in one trip.

We moved back into the house that I had built with my father and brother. It was old and decrepit, so we applied to the Hope Vale Council to build us a new four-bedroom house. The council agreed to our plan, which was to be built on the site of our old one. I did the work of knocking the old house down, even removing the stumps and clearing the area. We moved into the old people's hostel during this time. Peter Irwin, a local man from Cooktown, was the builder and the house was soon finished. Thelma meanwhile applied for a job at the hostel and worked as manager there for the next nine years.

Changes in Hope Vale's community spirit had been gradual, but were now noticeable to us because we had been away for so long. I have to go back in time here to the early seventies, when the consumption of alcohol was allowed in the community. In those first few years, this did not seem to have much of an impact on the communal life. Drug abuse came into people's lives in the 1980s. Then families started feuding and big mobs were fighting one another. It got bad when mobs started attacking individuals. The fights got dirty and were not fair any more. Those early violent times sowed the seeds for today's problems. It coincided with a vacuum of effective policing. Fortunately, the violence is not so bad these days. However, there is a great sense of loss of respect for others. There is a strong awareness now of the need for change, and people are setting up groups to make this possible. Good, effective and strong leadership is critical.

We became friends with Bill and Mavis Davenport, who were passionfruit growers. They suggested that Thelma and I grow passionfruit and so we decided to give it a go. We had a five-acre block on good red soil, the same block of land that Dad, Syd and I had cleared years ago. I was nearly sixty years old, but still strong. I could cut and lift posts onto a truck. We hired a truck for the posts and rails, and some young fellows brought them to

Myself with sisters Kathy and Dorothy, and brother Syd (my sister Ruth was absent that day).

our block. With a lot of effort, we got the trellises up and planted the passionfruit seedlings we had received from Bill Davenport. Bill and Mavis were a great help and our friendship deepened over the years. When we had finished, it was nearly Christmas and then the rains came. The vines flourished and the trellises were covered with fruit. We fertilised them and the fruit grew big. It was a great sight to see these healthy passionfruit hanging from the trellises! In that first harvest, we picked them ourselves. Bill and Mavis showed us where to get cartons. We sold some fruit and later bought a machine to push the fruit onto the table for cleaning and sorting into sizes. We had five years of growing passionfruit with good results, and all was going well.

Then a young fellow from Hope Vale came up to the block when it was due to be mowed and tossed a few matches here and there. Everything went up in flames. It was a big loss. We lost thousands of dollars in equipment, trellises, and plants, we had spent many hours of hard work establishing the orchard, and it was destroyed in an instant. At the court in Hope Vale, the boy got off scot-free.

We never went back to passionfruit farming but we kept our scrub garden from old times. There we already had pawpaws and bananas. We planted sugar bananas and Cavendish bananas. These we had to get rid of later by the Department of Primary Industry ruling, because of possible disease. We still have a good garden at the back of the house where we grow taros, pawpaws, bananas, mandarins, star apples, lychees, sapotes, custard apples and abiu, an exotic fruit from South America. It is true that what grows well in South America grows well here also.

George Rosendale was the pastor in Hope Vale. When George was released to go to Wonthulp, Walter Jack and I shared the ministry for two years. The next pastor was not inclined to give responsibility to bama, and this was a difficult time for me. I was disappointed that the training of bama had come to an end.

Land issues continued to play an important part in our lives, not always with happy results. In 1986, the Hope Vale Council was made a trustee for Deed of Grant in Trust (formerly Reserve) land. This was the first such grant in Queensland and was seen as a big breakthrough. Then the Mabo decision came in 1992. The Native Title Act was passed the following year. Hope Vale Native Title claims were recognised in 1997.

Aboriginal people have always belonged to the land. I was aiming to establish a sense of security, a sense of belonging, which we had lost along the line after our country was taken from us. We no longer felt we belonged anywhere and this feeling added to a growing sense of insecurity. I feel that this sense of insecurity has driven us away from our core, our sense of self. This has resulted in people becoming addicted to something, trying to fill the void they feel inside. I have always seen the land as our mother, a place and a presence where we might heal and grow. My vision was to have land in our traditional Binthi country.

I applied to ATSIC for the purchase of Mt Baird Station on Binthi land, and this was unsuccessful. Then I heard of the Indigenous Land Council and with help from our friends John Hill and Jo Wynter, we made another attempt. This was successful, and the first such acquisition on the Cape York Peninsula. I retained my vision that the land should be shared among all Binthi-Warra but the families could not agree. Dissent among clan members led to division of land into three separate parcels. I was not a participant in the dividing process and our family were given the middle section. The Woibos took the northern block and the Wallaces the southern block.

I was bitterly disappointed that we had been unable to manage the land cooperatively. My hopes are that future generations will be able to use the land, not only as an economic benefit but as a place for healing and spiritual renewal. I feel strongly

Belonging

'When I go to my land I feel relaxed and happy and I commune with nature. Being there gives me great joy. I feel I have come home, I belong. A feeling of not belonging somewhere adds to a feeling of insecurity. This is very important to address in land issues and reconciliation.'

that, to prevent misuse and division amongst the families, any economic benefit made from the land should be turned back into development of the land and facilities.

Mt Baird Station had been neglected for years and was overrun by the weed, sickle pod. Sickle pod forms impenetrable masses making it uninhabitable for native and farming animals. However, a combination of two exceptionally dry years and re-pasturing the property, had allowed clean paddocks of good grasses to grow. A few years after the acquisition of the station, I saw seven brolgas merrily walking on Mt Baird. It was such a happy sight. Brolgas are dancing birds respected by all Guugu Yimithirr. I have never heard of one of these birds being killed by any Guugu Yimithirr. When I saw the birds, I knew Mt Baird was back in balance. The Binthi-Warra had some of their land, so they were happy. I was happy. The brolgas were home and happy. Nature was back in balance again, so the country was happy. I took up my brushes and joyfully painted the dancing brolgas. This painting was given as a gift to the Indigenous Land Corporation.

In 1992, Wayne Rosendale applied for funding to go visit Stonehenge near Longreach to see my mother's country. We were eager to find more of our relatives in the region.

We hired a bus, which was filled with members of our families, all eager to see Nanny's country. We also had on board a new headstone for my sister Emily's grave at Woorabinda. It was a long trip out to far western Queensland. We went to Townsville, Charters Towers, then Hughenden where we met up with the Doolan family from Woorabinda, and on to Winton where we

Self-sufficiency
My father wrote down these words on our time of re-location from Woorabinda: 'How Muni wished that the government would only give the bama better and more suitable land, so that they could grow their own food. The young people ought to be very thankful that they are living on land where they can grow their own food and also sell some of it, when we older ones could not do so at Cape Bedford Mission.

Cockatoo

met more people, and then Longreach. It was late evening when we made camp at Longreach.

My mind went back to my mother's experience of travelling that distance from her home to Cape Bedford. It is a long, long way, much further than you think. When they were sent away, my mother Rachel was only ten years old, Dolly her sister was eight, and their little brother Harold was only six. They were the children who travelled the furthest of any to come to the Hope Valley mission.

Next day we headed out to Stonehenge. There were cattle stations everywhere. It was pastoral country, taken up with cattle and sheep runs. After Longreach it was about 150 more kilometres to Stonehenge. On the way there were signs to Warbreccan and Jundah, places I remember my Mum talking about. Then we came to Stonehenge.

Somehow the postmistress knew we were coming and gave us a warm welcome. We were surprised to find it was just a little shanty town, but it had been home to our mothers and grannies. My mother always spoke of fishing and netting with traditional nets on the Thompson River, just a stone's throw from the town. The water was murky in that part of the river, and there were little pools at the side. We got out and walked around, trying to imagine Mum, Auntie and Uncle there as children. We were there for a couple of hours. We dipped our hands in the water and rubbed it over our arms and faces. We bought some souvenirs in the shop. As we were leaving, Pastor George said to me, 'If that had been my mother, I would have plunged into the water, to remember my mother that way!'

Identity

This land is very important to me. It is somewhere that I can say I belong. Our connection to our land may be hard to explain, but this land gives so much to me. Its beauty and familiarity stirs me very deeply, it shares its creativity with me, its stories, its meaning, its flora and fauna.

Return to Hope Vale

Rachel and Dolly, third and fourth from the left

My mind went back to my mother's experience of travelling from her home to Cape Bedford. They were the children who travelled the furthest of any to come to the Hope Valley mission.

We drove back through to Barcaldine. This was wide country, full of sheep and horses. Here we were greeted by the Thompson family. My mother's maiden name was Thompson. We stayed at the Aboriginal hostel there. I used to go to meetings sometimes in Cairns and Rockhampton and I had met this man Thompson before. He was in charge of Aboriginal affairs in the Barcaldine area. A big fire was made and we had a good singalong.

The next day we passed through Jericho, Emerald, Dingo and then on to Duaringa. When I was working at Foleyvale I used to go through Duaringa. I remembered our flood crossing when we carried our luggage across the swollen creek on tea chests covered with tarpaulins.

Instead of going straight to Woorabinda, we went to Blackboy outstation which was a cattle run. The biggest surprise was the building we camped in. It was the same school building we had at Woorabinda. How they moved it there I don't know, but it brought back many memories.

As we drove into Woorabinda, memories came flooding back and brought tears to my eyes. The whole township was changed, with many more buildings. We were welcomed and given morning tea, and then we met up with some of the old people.

We called in at the cemetery to set up the headstone on Emily's grave. We had brought it in the bus with us, stowed carefully.

165

Cockatoo

The old wooden cross my father had made had withstood the weather, and was easy to find, and we knew Harold Wallace was buried beside her. But all the other grave markings were gone. It was sad to step on the ground where our loved ones were lying. I wished that my sisters Ruth and Dorothy had been able to come on this trip, but they were not well at that time. It was both a sad and a happy time to revisit Woorabinda, and see again the familiar places where we used to walk and play.

We took the road to Bauhinia Downs, where some of our men had worked as stockmen. Then we turned off to Monto and then Biloela, where they had gone cotton picking during the war. We passed through Gayndor where there are hot water springs and then came to Cherbourg. We stayed at the boarding house there. Our relations came there to talk with us and we had a good time together. They took us back to the emu farm which I had visited before with Henry Baru. From there we went to Rockhampton where we met up with some of my mother's relations. I hadn't been back to Woorabinda before, and it was a moving experience.

'Milgaannhaamaalmaa', Remembering, 2007

Our family in front of the gate to Stonehenge

We hired a bus, which was filled with members of our families, all eager to see Nanny's country. We also had on board a new headstone for my sister Emily's grave at Woorabinda.

At Emily's grave at Woorabinda

When I put the tombstone down on the grave, I started to cry and couldn't stop. When Emily died, we were sad but I was young and I didn't really grieve. At that moment everything came out.

Dynamic order #2, 2009

Doing art has become such a vital part of my life. It gives me purpose, a goal to always climb higher, see more and different things, to keep learning and to share important elements of my culture and learning.

CHAPTER ELEVEN

My art and my story

I never thought of myself as an artist until I got married. After my marriage, art brought in my bread and butter. I might not be doing art today if it wasn't for those art classes in Woorabinda with Mrs Jarrett. I used to draw stockmen sitting on a horse, or a bucking horse with someone on its back. She inspired me greatly, although she could be scotty at times! Dad wanted me to take on bark painting, so we got a stack of bark. He said I needed to keep going with my art. So Dad was another influence on me.

When I was working in Bundaberg, a lady from the Lutheran Church asked me if I knew anyone who could decorate a boomerang for her. I told her I would give it a go and she was very happy about that. She took me to the hardware shop and we got some acrylic paints in the traditional colours: red, yellow, black and white. I took the paints home and busied myself with the painting. When I finished and showed her the result she was very pleased and thought it was beautiful work.

In the late sixties, when I was still single, the Department of Aboriginal Affairs held art classes at Hope Vale. I attended with Tulo Gordon, Walter Jack, Johnny Allums, Kenny Walsh,

Godfrey Gordon, Benny McGreen, Martin James and some others. We used acrylics to paint landscapes and seascapes. I enjoyed learning about these new styles. In 1973 a tutor came to teach us portraiture and painting with oil paints.

In 1974 we went to a gathering at Lake Barrine on the Atherton Tablelands. People from Cape York, as far down as Edmonton, and across to the Northern Territory, had the privilege of doing a three-week art course with an Aboriginal Elder and famous artist, Wandjuk Marika, a Yirrakala man. This experience changed my life. I discovered a spiritual dimension to art. Before that, my work was inspired by ancient rock art and I used traditional colours based on natural pigments. Now I embraced the idea of contemporary art. I felt I might become a true artist.

At Lake Barrine, there were wonderful tutors. They encouraged us to experiment. We went for walks in the rainforest and watched the waterfalls and noted the difference between the peaceful water in the lake, and the bubbling, raging water in the falls. Lake Barrine is so beautiful and peaceful. It taught us the valuable lesson that you have to have peace within yourself. You need to picture yourself as a peaceful lake. Aggressive things destroy you completely. Only through peace can we develop in our artwork.

One of the tutors took us into the rainforest. We had to stand in a circle holding each others' hands. She told us that meditation is important in life. I regularly meditate to gain a fresh look on life, to acquire a fresh mind. You cannot be a good artist without a peaceful mind.

My good friend, Rodney Malloy was using his hands and painting straight onto the canvas without using a brush. He produced some beautiful contemporary art. Tulo Gordon and I met up with other friends from Woorabinda. Tulo was a great artist. Sambo Garby was another tutor. He did engraving on kettles. Tulo and Sambo Garby had worked around Gympie during the war. Wandjuk Marika showed us how to make brushes from hair. He taught us how to use our paintbrushes using a backward stroke. At the end of the course, an exhibition was held and a great deal of our work was sold.

My art and my story

Dynamic order #1, 2009

Our land gives us so much inspiration and learning. I trusted the land to inspire me to paint.

I went to my first TAFE course in 2000 with Walter Jack and others from Hope Vale. Over the years, we have taken courses in painting, drawing, pottery, screen printing, lino-cuts, etching, batik and working with ochre.

In 2001, I painted 'Spirit Realm' (see page 82), which I later entered in the Laura Art Award of 2003, winning first prize. In this painting, traditional symbols are depicted in an abstract form. This is an important painting to me as I see in it some of the abstract qualities I developed in my later work.

I won a scholarship from Arts Queensland to go to the University of South Queensland McGregor Summer School, held in Toowomba in 2003. Peter Griffin was our tutor. He had experience in working with Indigenous people and encouraged me in painting abstract art. This was a style I enjoyed experimenting with.

The second McGregor Summer School I attended was in 2006. My tutor was Geoff la Gerche. He had worked with Indigenous people in the Top End. I was hoping to do more abstract art, but Geoff was a landscape artist. I was interested in that too! I thought that he would teach me more about landscapes. Instead, he told me, 'Roy, your landscape is your Aboriginal art.' He left me with a huge canvas which I painted with a vivid orange abstract background superimposed with traditional Aboriginal motifs. I still consider this one of my best paintings. At the school I also did many small paintings, most of which were sold. Geoff encouraged me to be fearless with my use of colour. His greatest compliment was when he wrote to me recently and said, 'I think of you as one of my teachers.'

I have participated in many exhibitions: I have had my work on display in the Hope Vale exhibitions at the Tropical North Queensland TAFE College in Cairns and at the Tanks Art Centre in Cairns. I had an exhibition in Brisbane with Walter Jack, and my art was exhibited at the Sydney International Airport. My first solo exhibition was at Nature's Powerhouse in Cooktown in 2005. In 2007, I had my second solo exhibition at the Cairns Regional Gallery. The exhibition ran over the summer holidays and the opening was grand. I have had very good reviews.

I was involved in two important community projects in Cooktown. One was the creation of the Milbi Wall which tells our shared history from traditional times to the present day. It is a curved structure, representing the coils of the Rainbow Serpent, with our stories depicted in ceramic tiles. This was a major reconciliation project. The second project was the 'River of Life', in which scenes from the Endeavour River and its surrounds were depicted in ceramic tiles set in the pathway bordering the river between the wharf and the town. Like the Milbi Wall, this was a reconciliation project involving the whole community.

We were able to start an Art and Culture Centre in Hope Vale, using an old staff house, built when Uncle Roy Dick was foreman. This building has now been dismantled and the new Arts and Cultural Centre was built. We used the old police station while the new Arts and Cultural Centre was built. The old police station is an historical building that was built by Jack Bambi, a Thuupi man. Jack Bambi and a few others built the top part with bush timbers. Henry Baru did the cement works for it. Before we used it for our temporary Arts and Cultural Centre, our artists painted murals on the building's walls.

I have been serving as chairman for the Arts and Cultural Centre for some time. Since the signs requesting for permits to enter the community were taken down, Hope Vale started receiving more tourists. Unfortunately, more recently with the erection of the Alcohol Management Permit sign, tourist numbers have taken another plunge.

We have many gifted artists in this community. I would like to see us follow in Lockhart River's footsteps, where many of the artists have become internationally recognised.

In the early times, the old ladies used to weave and the men used to make artefacts. Hope Vale exported shadowboxes, nulla nullas, boomerangs, spears, clap sticks, bullroarers, didgeridoos and other artefacts. I would like to see this happen again with the younger generation getting involved. There have been many community projects at Hope Vale — the walls around the administration block have been painted with murals, as has the front wall of the new police-station. Another achievement is a series of panel screens at the entrance to the new health centre. These screens are traditional motifs etched onto anodised aluminium.

I believe I have not yet become a real professional artist, but I still enjoy it and I hope to be a good example for our young people. My children have shown great potential with the art they have produced, and I would be very proud if they were to continue.

I love the thought that this all started in the caves thousands of years ago. This rich cultural heritage can be an inspiration to us. One of my visions for the future is to bring back painting with ochre. We have a lot of ochre in this area. The colours are beautiful — black, yellow, light yellow, red and orange — all the natural colours. We just have to collect it. I have seen some lovely paintings that were made with ochre at the Cairns TAFE College.

I also love seeing the young people at Hope Vale dancing. I am strongly aware of the connection between dance and art in traditional society, and feel we should encourage them both in the community. The Hope Vale Art and Cultural Centre has always been a busy hub for cultural activities, strengthening relationships in the community. We preserve traditional knowledge and practices, and we can be innovative as well, using different mediums and techniques.

I believe that we are in this world for a purpose. Our purpose is not to destroy our body and mind through addictions. We each have to find our own purpose, which gives us an interest in life and brings enjoyment to our lives and that of others around us. Our older people passed on in their eighties, even in their nineties. They did not take anything to shorten their life, or ruin their body. Take an interest in doing something for life. Doing a good physical workout which brings on a good sweat gives you a great sense of satisfaction at the end of the day. Our balance will be restored when we find and pursue our good purpose in life. If you take life with confidence you can live life on life's terms. From living in a remote community, my own children have worked hard to achieve good outcomes. Ramona is an anthropologist, and Selwyn and Elroy are electricians.

Hopefully, my art and my story will inspire someone else to keep doing whatever may be their dream, their purpose in life. Everyone needs to find their purpose in life, for without that purpose we easily become drifters, not going anywhere much.

GUUGU YIMITHIRR GLOSSARY

The spelling of the Guugu Yimithirr words is based on phonetics, and therefore the spelling is variable. The glossary is written in the latest orthography agreed upon at the time of writing. A bit of interesting information is that the word kangaroo (gangurru) came from the Guugu Yimithirr language.

bama	Aboriginal person
babi	paternal grandmother
bayan	shelter, humpy
bayji	dilly bag
bigibigi	pig, wild pig
bigurrjirr	freshwater jewfish
binga thawuunh	person with same totem, totem itself
bithaaygu	few
bubu	ground, country
bulii!	fall down!
bulimun	policeman
buthu	tea-tree species with paper-like bark
buunhjaarr	minced stingray
buurraay	water
dagaarr manaa	adopt and raise a child
dawaar	star
dhulgan	sheoak
diwaan	scrub turkey
dunggan	friendly spirit
gadaar yugumalin	Bennett's tree kangaroo
gami	same-side grandparent: father's father, mother's mother
ganaa	alright, okay
gandaahl	shining
ganhaarr	crocodile
ganhil baathithil	traditional songs
granhthin	spirit
gulaan	possum
gunabal	strong or bad smell
gunbu gunbu	Christmas
gurrma	underground oven
guugu	speech, voice, word, language
maargami	fairy type creature, lives in the forest
mala-digarra	expert defender
manu-galga-thirr	ghostly creature
manyjal	mountain
matharr	incompetent, incapable, (bad hunter)
milbi	story
minha	meat
mirrgi	owlet nightjar
mugay	senior aunt or uncle
murrabal	barramundi
murrga	only, alone (emphatic), may be unsure
nanggurr	camp
ngalburrin	imprisoned
nganyja	initiation ceremony
ngathi	maternal grandfather
ngathiina	man's father-in-law
ngathu	mine
ngay	exclamation
ngayu	I, me, myself
ngurraarr	red-tailed black cockatoo
nguumbaal	initiated person, free of nganyja restrictions
nguunha	ghost, spirit
nguuthurr	daughter of woman, also used for 4th generation elder
thuga	orange-footed scrub hen
thugulga	mango bark
thuwan-ga	freshwater mussel
wandarr	white cockatoo
walaa!	look out!
walaan	good hunter
wambal	carpenter bird, large-tailed nightjar (Roy's totem)
wangaarr	white person
warra	resident of
wawu	spirit
wungguurrga	plains turkey
yiki	spirit, ghost
yimbaala	dance type, shake a leg dance
yimithirr	this way, like this
yumuurr	son or daughter

ACKNOWLEDGEMENTS

Many hands went into the creation of this book. Without the enormous input of the following individuals, this book would not have been possible: Margie Callaghan, Karien François who listened and helped write my story, and John Lang, who worked so hard on the original design of the book.

A special thank you to the staff at Magabala Books, Margaret Whiskin, Rachael Christensen and Simone Rice for wholeheartedly embracing *Cookatoo* with such tremendous enthusiasm. These women saw my story's potential – their professionalism, constant support, special efforts and growing intimate knowledge of the characters brought this book to life in the best way. So now we also are very excited.

Our gratitude extends to:
The Hopevale Arts and Cultural Learning Centre, which supported the project at all stages.

The Hopevale Council and Shirley Costello for giving access to many historical photographs.

Sebastian Gangel, Muni's great-grandson, who provided and allowed us to use valuable copies of photographs of the old missionary.

Eric Deeral
Professor Bruce Rigsby
Ellen White
Jo Wynter
Jan Howard
Jeanette Covacevich
Wil François-Wouters

And anyone we may have forgotten to mention.

Funding received from Queensland Government through Arts Queensland

Queensland Government